To A. W. Craver

The Psychiatry of
Robert Burton

Democritus   Junior

10   Now laſt of all to fill a place,
Preſented is the Authors face;
And in that habit which he weares,
His Image to the world appeares.
His minde no art can well expreſſe,
That by his writings you may gueſſe.
It was not pride, nor yet vaineglory,
(Though others doe it commonly)

Made him doe this: if you muſt know,
The Printer would needs haue it ſo.
Then doe not frowne or ſcoffe at it,
Deride not, or detract a whit.
For ſurely as thou doſt by him,
He will doe the ſame againe.
Then looke vpon't, behold and ſee,
As thou likeſt it, ſo it likes thee.

The Psychiatry of
Robert Burton

by BERGEN EVANS
in consultation with
GEORGE J. MOHR, M.D.

OCTAGON BOOKS

A DIVISION OF FARRAR, STRAUS AND GIROUX

New York   1972

Copyright, 1944, Columbia University Press
Copyright renewed, 1972, Columbia University Press

Reprinted 1972
by special arrangement with Columbia University Press

OCTAGON BOOKS
A DIVISION OF FARRAR, STRAUS & GIROUX, INC.
19 Union Square West
New York, N. Y. 10003

Library of Congress Cataloging in Publication Data

Evans, Bergen, 1904-
    The psychiatry of Robert Burton.
    Bibliography: p.
    1. Melancholy. 2. Burton, Robert, 1577-1640. 3. Burton, Robert,
1577-1640. The anatomy of melancholy. I. Title.

PR2224.E9   1972   616.8'9   72-4487
ISBN 0-374-92638-7

Printed in U.S.A. by
NOBLE OFFSET PRINTERS, INC.
NEW YORK, N.Y. 10003

Preface

It is now more than three hundred years since Robert Burton shipwrecked his life upon "the vile rock of melancholy" and decided to devote the salvaged remnants of it to anatomizing the dark humor that had ruined him. He wrote of melancholy, he said, "by being busy to avoid melancholy" and sought "to show the causes, symptoms, and several particular cures, that it may be the better avoided . . . moved thereunto for the generality of it, and to do good, it being a disease so frequent as few there are that feel not the smart of it."

The early seventeenth century was a period of great intellectual turmoil. The old world of the theologians was plainly crumbling, and the new world of the scientists had not yet assumed sufficient clarity of outline to offer its specious hopes. What had been accepted for thousands of years as permanent, unalterable reality was perceived with amazement to have been only a creation—or at best an interpretation—of the human mind.

Serious men were, therefore, passionately interested in the human mind, particularly in what today is complacently called "abnormal" psychology, and Burton's book spoke to their hearts. The first, second, and third editions, he tells us, "were suddenly gone, eagerly read." Five editions appeared in his lifetime and three more within a generation of his death. If one may judge by the frequency of publication, *The Anatomy of Melancholy* was almost three times as popular as Shakespeare's plays.

And then, as the world gradually assumed a reassuring appearance in the light of science, most men forgot the basic irrationality of things, took the images of the mind for external reality, and ceased to probe the darkest enigma of all—the mind that makes all else seem clear. Burton's folios gathered dust and sank to the shilling stalls in the second-hand markets. Their author became a shadowy remembrance.

In the nineteenth century interest in the *Anatomy* revived, but it was adventitious, centering almost entirely upon its curious lore and the "quaintness" of its style. One would certainly have expected Byron, for instance, with his own neurotic troubles, to have sensed something of the book's true import; yet, although he read it a great deal, it was to him merely an entertaining commonplace book "most useful to a man who wishes to acquire the reputation of being well read with the least trouble." Even at the end of the century a critic as astute as Barrett Wendell could label it a "treasury of oddities" and say with academic assurance, "You do not know quite what it all means; you have no reason to believe that he knows any better than you."

By the twentieth century Burton's subject was fashionable again, but he was not re-established as a serious thinker. His romantic admirers had damned him more thoroughly than the passage of time; psychologists had enough to cope with in the orthodoxies of the day without investigating anything avowedly quaint.

One or two voices were raised to suggest that he might have something to say to a world which had become interested in psychology again, but they were faint and their suggestions passed unheeded. In 1914 Sir William Osler, writing in the *Yale Review*, called the *Anatomy* "a medical treatise, the greatest indeed written by a layman," and made a plea for a serious consideration of its psychiatric value, but 1914 was an inauspicious year for such a proposal. In 1936 Dr. Joseph Miller published a short article on Burton in the *Annals of Medical History* in which he acknowledged, though he did not take time to show, that the *Anatomy* deserved a place in the history of medicine. These two brief mentions, however, constitute the only attention which Burton has received from medical writers in the twentieth century.

It is the purpose of the following pages to present Robert Burton's theories of psychiatry and to evaluate them in the light of modern psychological knowledge.

Although every edition of the *Anatomy* published in Burton's lifetime has been consulted, particularly the first posthumous edition, the sixth, the quotations from the *Anatomy* in this book (except one—which is clearly marked) are taken, for the reader's convenience, from the edition "modernized" by Floyd Dell and Paul Jordan-Smith and published in one volume by Farrar and Rinehart in 1927. We are indebted to the publishers of that work for permission to make such copious use of it.

All quotations in this book which are not designated as drawn from some other source are from *The Anatomy of Melancholy*.

BERGEN EVANS

Evanston, Illinois
January 30, 1944

Contents

The Man

THERE is a legend that the merriment of the philosopher Democritus, particularly his habit of laughing aloud on solemn occasions, caused his fellow townsmen, the citizens of Abdera, in Thrace, to doubt his sanity and to summon Hippocrates to examine him. It is true that Democritus had always been peculiar in this respect; at the moment of his birth, it was said, he had looked about him and then burst into a peal of laughter. But the tendency had increased so disturbingly with the passage of years that the Abderites felt that medical attention was imperative.

An account of the interview between the philosopher and the physician is ascribed to Hippocrates himself, in the so-called Epistle to Damagetus.[1] He found the philosopher, he said, "a little, wearyish old man," seated in his garden reading a book on abnormal psychology and surrounded by the carcasses of various animals which he had been dissecting "to find out the seat of this black bile, or melancholy, whence it proceeds, and how it was engendered in men's bodies," that he might cure it in himself and teach others how to avoid it.

Hippocrates sought to open the interview amiably by commending this purpose and expressing envy of the leisure which left him free to pursue such studies. Instead of being flattered, Democritus seemed to be irritated. Why, he asked sharply, was it necessary for Hippocrates to envy other men's leisure? Did he not have the same amount of time that all people have? Hippoc-

[1] The Epistle to Damagetus has been shown to be spurious. But that does not matter here, since we are concerned with its import to Burton, who believed it. The translation followed is his. See *The Anatomy of Melancholy*, ed. by Floyd Dell and Paul Jordan-Smith, pp. 38–42.

rates answered that his time was taken up with domestic affairs. He had a wife and children to maintain and the expenses of a household to meet. Then there were the obligations of friendship and neighborliness and the unavoidable calamities of sickness and death. The combined exactions of all these things left little leisure for study.

At this, Democritus laughed profusely, and when Hippocrates asked him why he laughed he answered that he laughed at one more evidence of human folly, at one more instance of the sacrificing of the ends of life for the means. The confusion of values in the human mind, he said, was ludicrous. Men are ambitious and make sacrifices—but for what? They take such infinite pains— to increase their pains. They dig deep mines in the earth, seeking for gold wherewith to increase their pleasures but finding, usually, only death. They are violent and inconsistent. Some seek to be obeyed in many provinces, yet will themselves obey in none. Some men give up all to marry women whom they soon hate and forsake. Some spend vast sums to educate their children, only to despise and neglect them after they are educated. Millions give their lives to the pursuit of riches; few obtain them, and fewer still enjoy them.

To folly they add viciousness. Truth and justice are unknown among mankind. Every family is torn with dissension; every man and woman is a greedy competitor with his or her nearest kin. Inanimate things are of value only in so far as they serve human beings, yet most men seem to attach value to material objects and at the same time to hate their fellow men. Everywhere men profess certain ideals and yet, without seeming awareness of the contradiction, govern their actions by principles which they condemn. The kindest explanation for this state of affairs was that all men were disordered in their minds.

Hippocrates agreed with much of what Democritus said, but could not agree that it was ludicrous. Men are the slaves of necessity, he protested; they are moved by their passions, not their minds. No man can foresee the future, yet every man must act on the assumption that he can. Circumstances change, and the wisest courses may end in disaster. Men act for the best and seek those ends which they think will bring happiness. Most fail, it is true, because of frail judgment or adverse circumstances, but surely this is no justification for laughter.

At this Democritus "laughed again aloud, perceiving he wholly mistook him, and did not well understand what he had said concerning perturbations and tranquillity of the mind." It was not, he said, the futility of men's actions that amused him, but their inability to see their true state or to govern themselves with discretion. Their misfortunes were, indeed, no just grounds for reproach, but their egotism and self-assurance in the face of these misfortunes were. They seem utterly unable to learn from the experiences of others; each man has to run the entire gamut of folly for himself. They tumble headlong into many calamities from mere arrogant lack of attention. They remain children all their days, being unable, it would seem, to accept the limitations that external reality imposes.

Doth it not deserve laughter [he demanded] to see an amorous fool torment himself for a wench; weep, howl for a misshapen slut, a dowdy, sometimes, that might have his choice of the finest beauties? Is there any remedy for this in physick? I do anatomize and cut up these poor beasts, to see these distempers, vanities, and follies, yet such proof were better made on man's body, if my kind nature would endure it: who from the hour of his birth is most miserable, weak, and sickly; when he sucks he is guided by others, when he is grown great practiseth unhappiness, and is sturdy, and when old, a child again, and repenteth him of his past life.

He was here interrupted by one that brought him books, but recovering the thread of his discourse he continued his tirade, insisting that all men were mad.

To prove my former speeches [he went on], look into courts, or private houses. Judges give judgement according to their own advantage, doing manifest wrong to poor innocents to please others. Notaries alter sentences, and for money lose their deeds. Some make false monies, others counterfeit false weights. Some abuse their parents, yea corrupt their own sisters, others make long libels and pasquils, defaming men of good life, and extol such as are lewd and vicious. Some rob one, some another; magistrates make laws against thieves, and are the veriest thieves themselves. Some kill themselves, others despair, not obtaining their desires. Some dance, sing, laugh, feast and banquet, whilst others sigh, languish, mourn and lament, having neither meat, drink, nor clothes. Some prank up their bodies, and have their minds full of execrable vices. . . . Women are all day a dressing, to pleasure other men abroad, and go like sluts at home, not caring to please their own husbands whom they should. Seeing men are so fickle, so sottish, so intemperate, why should not I laugh at those, to whom folly seems wisdom, will not be cured, and perceive it not? [2]

Thus he continued talking throughout the afternoon and until late in the evening. Melancholy and madness, he declared, warming to his particular theme, differed only in degree; and madness, in its lighter forms, was universal. So that if he could but find the seat of melancholy and the remedy for it, he would have rendered mankind the greatest of all possible services.

Hippocrates listened entranced, and when he finally came away he told the Abderites that, notwithstanding his vagaries, "the world had not a wiser, a more learned, or a more honest man" than Democritus, and that "they were much deceived to say that he was mad."

Two thousand years later another little, wearyish old man determined to "revive, prosecute and finish" the quest which he believed Democritus had begun and Hippocrates had praised. He was Robert Burton, a fellow of Christ Church, in Oxford, who, under the pseudonym of Democritus Junior, published in 1621 *The Anatomy of Melancholy*, or, as we would say, *An Analysis of Melancholia*.

Burton was by profession a divine, but by inclination a physician; which, as he himself observed, was not a bad combination for one who would study a disease that is of both soul and body and of neither separately. That he devoted his life to the study of mental aberration and was concerned with no other branch of

[2] *Ibid.*, pp. 41–42.

medicine, except in so far as it bore on his central interest, entitles him, perhaps, to be regarded as one of the first psychiatrists.

Of his life tantalizingly little is known. He was born at Lindley, in Leicestershire, the fourth of nine children, in 1577. On the engraved title page of his brother's *Description of Leicestershire* Lindley is represented as a handsome estate, with a considerable park or garden, the whole enclosed by a moat. And we are told in the course of the work that it was a pleasant and fertile spot. Both brothers make much of their distinguished ancestry, though the greatest single accomplishment that William, the author of the *Description,* can attribute to any of his forebears is the procuring by his grandmother's father of "the advantage of the grounde, winde and sunne" for Henry of Richmond at Bosworth Field.

Robert is content with the more general statement that he came "of worshipful parents, in an ancient family," and even this he immediately qualifies with the bitter reflection that, since he is a younger brother, such matters don't concern him. Of his mother he states only that she had "excellent skill in chirurgery, sore eyes, aches, etc.," wherewith she performed "many famous and good cures upon divers poor folks that were otherwise destitute of help."

That there was a neurotic strain in the family is suggested by the account which William gives of their mother's brother, Anthony Faunt, a man "of a comely and graceful personage, pleasing countenance, and good gesture, of great valor and courage, having a pleasant wit and good judgement." So endowed he had become a public figure, serving as Justice of the Peace and later as High Sheriff of Leicester. The dignity and splendor of these offices appealed to him, and in 1588, at the threat of the Spanish Armada, he had the honor to be chosen Lieutenant General of all the forces of the shire. "But being crossed in this," his nephew adds, "by Henry Earl of Huntington, Lord Lieutenant for the County (who . . . appointed for that service his brother Master Walter Hastings of Kirby) [he] fell into so great a passion of

melancholy, that within a short time after he died in the said year
1588." ³

Another uncle, Arthur Faunt, ran away to the continent when
he was fourteen years old, became a Jesuit, "and never returned
into this land."

Of Burton's mother it is to be wished that we had more information. To effect "many famous and good cures upon divers poor
folks that were otherwise destitute of help" was a definite part
of the duties of a lady of the manor, and it would be unwarrantable to assume solely from Mistress Dorothy Burton's activities in
this sort that she was an aggressive woman, antipathetic to her
retiring and diffident son. But the detail does fit into such an assumption, more especially as Burton says that her skill, or at least her
activity, was unusual and widely known. And it is significant that
this statement occurs in a passage in which he is apologizing to
her memory for having formerly thought one of her cures "most
absurd and ridiculous." She had been accustomed, he says, to
treat an ague by the application of an amulet "of a Spider in a
nutshell lapped in silk," a procedure which he had regarded with
contempt "till at length, rambling amongst authors," he had found
"this very medicine in Dioscorides, approved by Matthiolus, repeated by Aldrovandus, in his chapter on Spiders." Whereupon
he began "to have a better opinion of it"—and of his mother! ⁴

The assumption that she was domineering and unaffectionate toward him—or at least that he thought she was—is supported by the
intensity of feeling with which he so often alludes in the *Anatomy*
to the cruelty and indifference of parents. A little child must have
more than milk, he says, for instance, in a sudden passionate aside,
in his section on diet; he must have love and kindness as well, and
an affectionate wet nurse is always to be preferred to an unfeeling
mother.

At any rate, whatever the cause, Burton had an unhappy childhood. He speaks of his schooldays with loathing: "There is no
slavery in the world like to that of a grammar scholar." When a

³ William Burton, *The Description of Leicestershire*, p. 105.
⁴ *Anatomy*, pp. 596–597, *passim*.

boy, he confesses, he had become discouraged; he had been "a broken spirit," his teachers had not loved him, and he had "moped, many times weary of life."

Whether he was actually neglected or mistreated it is now impossible to discover. Nor does the reality greatly matter. What does matter, when it comes to interpreting his book, is that early in life he presented the signs of a depressive character and that he felt he had been denied affection.

In 1593 he matriculated at Brasenose College in Oxford. Practically all that is known of his college career are the dates of his matriculation and graduation. And even in them lurks a mystery. For he did not receive his B.A. until 1602, and then not from Brasenose but from Christ Church, to which he had transferred in 1599. He was thus twenty-six when he graduated, as against the usual age of nineteen or younger.

What was he doing between 1593 and 1599? Did he suffer from some serious illness, perhaps a long period of depression? He himself hints at this explanation. He had once been active and ambitious, he says, but the ship of his hopes had been fatally driven upon the rock of melancholy and he had withdrawn forever from the active world, to live "a silent, sedentary, solitary life in the University," stewing in his own "domestic discontents" and —although he does not say so directly—gazing enviously from his study window upon the lives of happier men.

Though he spent his entire life as a fellow in Oxford, he has little good to say of the academic life or of those who follow it. The gown of the collegian was "the ensign of his infelicity." He had played for safety and won it, but he never ceased to regret the bright and dangerous world which his fears had led him to renounce.

His scorn for scholars knows no bounds. They are a servile lot, he sneers, prostituting themselves "as fiddlers or mercenary tradesmen, to serve great men's turns for a small reward." They cringe and whine to their patrons "and for hope of gain . . . flatter with hyperbolical eulogiums" some "illiterate unworthy idiot . . . whom they should rather vilify and rail at for his no-

torious villainies and vices." They have a certain store of knowledge, he admits, but it is useless, and in practical matters, in the
things that count in life, they are like children; "they can measure
the heavens, range over the world, teach others wisdom, and yet,
in bargains and contracts, they are circumvented by every base
tradesman." [5]

Under this scorn there is resentment, resentment for the neglect
with which he felt he had been treated. Learning and ability, he
says bitterly, count for nothing in this world; bribery and cor-
ruption carry everything before them. Honesty and integrity are
only liabilities. This is the burden of his song. The obsequious
cleric who has no true principles, but cuts his cloth according to
his master's coat, is the man who gains advancement:

whilst in the mean time we that are University men, like so many hide-
bound calves in a pasture, tarry out our time, wither away as a flower
ungathered in a garden, & are never used: or, as too many candles,
illuminate ourselves alone, obscuring one another's light, & are not
discerned here at all, the least of which, translated to a dark room, or
to some Country Benefice, where it might shine apart, would give a
fair light, and be seen over all. Whilst we lie waiting here, as those sick
men did at the pool of Bethesda, till the Angel stirred the water, ex-
pecting a good hour, they step between, and beguile us of our preferment. I have not yet said. If after long expectation, much expence, tra-
vail, earnest suit of ourselves and friends, we obtain a small Benefice at
last, our misery begins afresh; we are suddenly encountered with the
flesh, world, and Devil, with a new onset; we change a quiet life for an
ocean of troubles, we come to a ruinous house, which, before it be
habitable, must be necessarily (to our great damage) repaired; we are
compelled to sue for dilapidations, or else sued ourselves, and, scarce
yet settled, we are called upon for our predecessor's arrearages; first
fruits, tenths, subsidies, are instantly to be paid, benevolence, procura-
tions, &c., and, which is most to be feared, we light upon a crackt
title. . . . Or else we are insulted over and trampled on by domineering officers, fleeced by those greedy Harpies to get more fees; we stand

[5] *Ibid.*, p. 265. See all of Part I, Sec. 2, Memb. 3, Subs. 15, "The Miseries of
Scholars."

in fear of some precedent lapse; we fall amongst refractory, seditious sectaries, peevish Puritans, perverse Papists, a lascivious rout of Atheistical Epicures, that will not be reformed, or some litigious people, (*those wild beasts of Ephesus* must be fought with), that will not pay their dues without much repining, or compelled by long suit; for the generality of laymen despise the clergy,—an old axiom; all they think well gotten that is had from the Church, and by such uncivil harsh dealings they make their poor Minister weary of his place, if not his life: and put case they be quiet honest men, make the best of it, as often it falls out, from a polite and terse Academick he must turn rustick, rude, melancholise alone, learn to forget; or else, as many do, become Malsters, Graziers, Chapmen, &c. . . . and daily converse with a company of idiots and clowns.[6]

This is not the worst. The university man may be reduced to "trencher Chaplain" in some country house, "crouching to a rich chuff for a meal's meat." And when he is decrepit, when, like his counterpart the ass, he has worn out his time for provender and sold his self-respect into the bargain ("for a Falconer's wages"), he may be retired to some beggarly living on condition that he marry a poor kinswoman of his patron's or, perchance, a cast-off mistress, some "crackt chambermaid."

Burton confesses that he had once himself been so mad "as to bussell abroad and seek out preferment." But he had been too modest, he says; he lacked the necessary effrontery. "Had I done as others did, put myself forward, I might have haply been as great a man as many of my equals . . . [but] I had no money, I wanted impudence, I could not scramble, temporize, dissemble." His sermons, he felt, were as good as the best, but he scorned to publish them, as was then the fashion, to exalt himself into notice: "I have ever been as desirous to suppress my labours in this kind, as others have been to press and publish theirs." There were already "so many books in that kind, so many commentators, treatises, pamphlets, expositions, sermons, that whole teams of oxen cannot draw them."

[6] *Ibid.*, pp. 277–278. Fielding's picture of Parson Trulliber (*Joseph Andrews*, Bk. 2, chap. xiv) shows that Burton's gloom was not groundless.

Had I been as forward and ambitious as some others, I might have haply printed a Sermon at Paul's Cross, a Sermon in St. Mary's, Oxford, a Sermon in Christ-Church, or a Sermon before the Right Honourable, Right Reverend, a Sermon before the Right Worshipful, a Sermon in Latin, in English, a Sermon with a name, a Sermon without, a Sermon, a Sermon, &c.[7]

But he will none of them. If these are the means to preferment, he will remain unpreferred. He is through, he says. He will tire himself and trouble his friends no more. He compares himself to a mired horse that has struggled at first with all its might and main but now, seeing that there is no remedy, lies still. He may even abandon the academic life altogether and become a miller or sell ale, "as some have done."

Such is the gloomy tenor of his own account of his life and fortunes. But the facts, as we know them, do not seem to justify quite so much bitterness. His intellectual worth, so Anthony Wood was told later by those who had known him, was recognized from the beginning. He was regarded as a most promising student, the usual teaching arrangements, in his case, being considered as a mere formality, since it was felt that he needed no teacher. While he was yet a student he had the distinction of being made the college librarian. Immediately after graduation he was appointed to a fellowship, and subsequently, at different times, he obtained two livings, which he held, in addition to his fellowship, "with much ado to his dying day." [8] Three times he was appointed clerk of the market in Oxford—not a great honor, to be sure, but certainly an indication that his associates regarded him as a man of affairs. Eighteen times during his years at Oxford he published Latin verses in the various college or university publications. A satirical play, *Philosophaster*, which he had written in 1606 was acted at Christ Church in 1617 and was received with applause. When he was in his middle forties he published what became, almost at once, one of the most popular books of the age. It had a phenomenal sale and brought him fame and wealth. He was es-

[7] *Anatomy*, p. 27.   [8] Wood, *Athenae Oxonienses*, I, 627.

teemed by those among whom he lived, and his acquaintance was sought by the great of the land.

Surely this is not an unfavorable balance sheet as human lives go. The basis of his disappointment must be sought in the excess of his expectations rather than in the meagerness of his accomplishments.

He died on the twenty-fifth of January, 1640, so near to the exact time that he had for years predicted that it was whispered that he had hanged himself to prove a prophet. Nor can this be entirely dismissed as an undergraduate witticism, for on his tomb, at his own request, was triumphantly inscribed the nativity which he had calculated and confirmed. And the rumor is further supported by the cryptic epitaph which he had composed and which, also at his request, was carved under his bust in Christ Church cathedral:

Paucis Notus Paucioribus Ignotus
Hic Iacet
Democritus Iunior
Cui Vitam Dedit et Mortem
Melancholia

—"Known to few, unknown to fewer, here lies Democritus Junior, to whom melancholy gave both life and death." [9]

The *Paucis Notus* seems to mean, "I, Robert Burton, am known to few because I am a recluse." And anyone familiar with the temper of *The Anatomy of Melancholy* will feel that there is the added implication that such obscurity was an injustice and a plain illustration of the world's ingratitude and unwillingness to recognize merit. The *Paucioribus Ignotus* is more obscure, being, indeed, the heart of the mystery and, possibly, not intended to have any exact meaning. It is usually assumed to be a reference to his fame as an author, and such it may be, though Burton was not given to open and direct boasting. It may well, however, have had

[9] A photograph of the effigy bust, the nativity, and the epitaph serves as the frontispiece to Paul Jordan-Smith's *Bibliographia Burtoniana*.

a more recondite meaning: "but that which I really am, a melancholy man, an unloved man, is unknown to even fewer than the few who know me—because nothing is commoner, in this unfeeling world, than to be unloved and rejected." The "life" that melancholy gave was, no doubt, the great intellectual interest that had filled his days and made them supportable. The "death" may have been a continual depression of spirits that robbed life of its joy. Or it may have been suicide.

Burton bequeathed his library of more than a thousand volumes (then an extraordinary collection for a private individual) to the library of Christ Church and to the Bodleian. It was noted that a great many of his books "were little historicall diverting pamphlets, now grown wonderfull scarce, which Mr. Burton used to divert himself with, as he did with other little merry books, of which there are many in his benefaction, one of which is *The History of Tom Thumb*." [10]

His effigy bust depicts him in a ruff and gown, with a round face, short white beard and moustache, close-cropped white hair above a high forehead, wide-set eyes, and an expression in which a tendency to laugh appears to be held in suppression by sadness. His best-known representation, the portrait on Le Blon's famous engraved title page in the third edition of the *Anatomy*, 1628, is too small and in most copies too worn to suggest anything except that it must have been a fair likeness. The portrait in the 1632 edition is reproduced as a frontispiece to this volume.

Anthony Wood, who as a child may have seen Burton and as a man was acquainted with many who had known him well, gives this character of him:

He was an exact Mathematician, a curious [careful] Calculator of Nativities, a general read Scholar, a thro'-pac'd Philologist, and one that understood the surveying of Lands well. As he was by many accounted a severe student, a devourer of Authors, a melancholy and humerous [crotchety] Person; so by others, who knew him well, a Person of great honesty, plain dealing and Charity. I have heard some of the Antients of *Ch. Ch.* often say, that his Company was very merry, facete

[10] Hearne, *Reliquiae Hearnianae*, ed. by Philip Bliss, p. 798.

and juvenile, and no Man in his time did surpass him for his ready and dextrous interlarding his common discourses among them with Verses from the Poets, or Sentences from classical Authors. Which being then all the fashion in the University, made his Company more acceptable.[11]

Hearne, who speaks of Burton as "one of the most facetious and pleasant companions of that age," may have been echoing Wood, but the additional information that his conversation "was very innocent" suggests that he had an additional source. Hearne lived almost a hundred years later than Burton, but anecdotes of eccentric dons have always been good in Oxford for at least a century. One of them constitutes Hearne's only other mention of Burton:

The earl of Southampton went into a shop and inquired of the bookseller for Burton's "Anatomy of Melancholly." Mr. Burton sate in a corner of the shop at that time. Says the bookseller, My lord, if you please, I can shew you the author. He did so. *Mr. Burton*, says the earl, *your servant. Mr. Southampton*, says Mr. Burton, *your servant*, and away he went.[12]

Trifling as this incident is, it is not without interest. Hearne sees it as a piece of whimsicality, the embarrassed modesty of a "humorous" man. He assumes that Burton did not like to be praised by anyone, however great or gracious. And so it may have been. But it is possible to read another meaning into the act; rather than modesty, Burton's conduct suggests arrogance, the arrogance underlying a depressive character. He plainly knew the identity of the man who had spoken to him. An earl was then a very great man, and this particular earl was a cultured and accomplished man to boot. His introduction of himself was presumably intended as an act of courteous homage. Yet Burton, for all his "plain dealing and charity," rebuffed it with deliberate rudeness. For the use of "Mr." to an earl in the seventeenth century could have been interpreted only as an impertinence or a very strange "humor." To a modern observer it seems likely that it was the former masquerading as the latter, and the sudden departure a precipitate

[11] *Athenae Oxonienses*, I, 628. [12] *Reliquiae Hearnianae*, p. 288.

retreat from the possible consequences of his own boldness. Burton appears to have been carried away by a sudden flood of resentment against the aristocrat who could thus patronize him by a compliment, and his compensatory bit of acting betrays how near the surface his aggressive feelings lay, how intolerant he was of anyone in a favored position which he, the "unloved child," secretly coveted.

Bishop Kennett, in a marginal note in his *Register and Chronicle*, records another curious legend. And this, together with Hearne's story and Wood's account and Aubrey's brief statement that it was believed he had committed suicide, makes up the all-too-meager memorials of Burton that survive.

The author [Kennett says, after mentioning the *Anatomy*] is said to have labored long in the Writing of this Book to suppress his own Melancholy, and yet did but improve it. . . . In an interval of Vapours he could be extreamly pleasant, and raise laughter in any Company. Yet I have heard that nothing at last could make him laugh, but going down to the Bridge-foot in Oxford, and hearing the barge-men scold and storm and swear at one another, at which he would set his Hands to his sides, and laugh most profusely: Yet in his College and Chamber so mute and mopish that he was suspected to be Felo de se.[13]

This peculiar diversion was, obviously, a studied and somewhat theatrical imitation of Democritus, who (so Burton tells us) used to refresh himself, whenever *he* was weary, by going down to the harbor at Abdera and laughing at what he saw there; and to Bishop Kennett, and to many other writers who have repeated his story, it is a droll instance of the length to which Burton went in his efforts to pattern himself after his illustrious forerunner.

But the imitation was not wholly perfect. Democritus went to the harbor because that was the busy part of Abdera, the commercial part, and it was there that the vanity of human pursuits, at which he laughed, was most evident. It is true that the Thames, hardly more than a creek, with its barges, hardly more than rowboats, represented whatever harbor Oxford could show, but the

[13] Kennett, *A Register and Chronicle*, I, 320–321, margin.

parallel would have been better, as far as significance goes, had Burton gone to Carfax, the commercial center of the town, or to St. Giles's Fair.

The quarrelsome, swearing bargees, however, probably represented a virile world from which he felt himself apart and yet with which, momentarily, he could by this little adventure in some small measure identify himself. They were not part of dull, pedantic Oxford, but visitors from the glamorous outer world, profane and energetic, and by laughing with them, thus ostentatiously, he could serve notice on the "hide-bound calves" that he, at least, was a man.

Such are the slight biographical details that have been preserved. A few more are supplied by Burton himself in the course of the *Anatomy*. He mentions briefly his father, three of his brothers, and, as has been said, his mother. He tells us where he was born and remembers with delight the pleasant air and the delightful view from a hill behind the house. He speaks with loathing of his school days and grumbles eternally at Oxford. He assures us that his life has been free from the breath of scandal. He is even an ascetic, a water drinker all his life.

In occasional parentheses and asides he tells us of his pleasures. Like Democritus he loved gardening, but the greatest of all his delights was reading in his chambers "sweetened with the smoke of juniper." He delighted in mathematics and in cartography. He had never traveled "but in Map or Card," but in that particular form of traveling no man had ever gone farther. The whole wonderful third Member of the second Section of the second Part, "Air Rectified. With a digression of the Air," is a rhapsody on the pleasures of cosmography, "wherein I freely expatiate and exercise myself for my recreation." He longs to be some long-winged hawk that he may leave his dull study and, soaring aloft, see for himself those rarities and wonders of which the voyagers tell.

He speaks proudly of the breadth of his interests, perhaps in defiance of his sedate colleagues, who, no doubt, raised their eyebrows at his superficial versatility. He has no desire, he declares, "to be a slave of one science," but prefers "to rove abroad . . . to have an oar in every man's boat, to taste of every dish, and sip of every cup," though he confesses, disarmingly, that this may be just another name for diffuseness and want of settled purpose, an excuse for "a running wit, an unconstant, unsettled mind." He does not pretend to be methodical; he has, rather, approached his work "like a ranging spaniel, that barks at every bird he sees, leaving his game." "I have followed all," he cheerfully admits, "saving that which I should. . . . I have read many books, but to little purpose, for want of good method; I have confusedly tumbled over divers authors in our Libraries, with small profit, for want of art, order, memory, judgement." [14]

He grants his tendency to melancholia. In fact he rather glories in it. It is a mark of distinction: "Melancholy advanceth men's conceits [imaginations], more than any other humour whatsoever"; "the most generous spirits and the finest wits are subject to it"; and "there is no great genius without a touch of madness." It had certainly furnished him with motive and material for his book.

So much he tells us directly about himself and more may be gathered by inference. It is interesting, for example, that although he lists and describes innumerable symptoms of melancholia he does not list or describe one which he *demonstrates* on almost every page—namely, continual self-depreciation. The rejection which he had experienced or imagined in childhood seems to have set the pattern for his whole life: nobody loves him; nothing that he does or is a part of has any true value; he has no learning, no ability, no mental powers at all; even his book, the work of his lifetime, is not his, but only a jumble of other men's thoughts awkwardly raked together.

We find much the same thing in Chaucer, the English writer with whose works Burton seemed to be most familiar. But there is a marked difference in the nature of the two men's self-abasement. When Chaucer states that he has little wit and that his opinions are not important one feels that, despite the fre-

14 *Anatomy*, p. 13.

quently obvious irony, he is being quietly sincere. Something in
his manner carries a conviction of genuine humility. There is a
serenity and a good-humored acceptance of things as they are
that would have been impossible, one feels, had he secretly felt
himself and his own concerns to be of prime importance. The
most dreadful scoundrels, the most selfish stupidity, and the most
arrogant ignorance elicit merely a gentle, mocking smile as he
exposes them. Only on the rarest occasions does he permit himself a quiet word of disapproval.

But that Burton's self-depreciation does not represent a sincere
and reasoned opinion of himself is shown in the ferocity with
which, in hundreds of passages, he attacks all who disagree with
him. He, too, professes to be a man of limited powers and restricted knowledge, but, unlike Chaucer, he has no toleration for
those who dare to think otherwise than he does. At every difference of opinion Chaucer is quick to suggest that he may be wrong,
that his opponents have probably given the matter more thought
than he is capable of, and so forth, and under the jesting there is a
clear note of quiet sincerity in all this. But nothing of the sort is
ever heard from Burton; on the contrary he hurls avalanches
of billingsgate, spouts whole Vesuviuses of vituperation upon all
who oppose him in any matter whatever.

It is hard to accept his anonymity as a sincere and modest wish
to remain unknown. He protests too much; he says that he will
not reveal his name; if the reader insists on knowing who wrote
the book, why it was the man in the moon. Yet he signed his name
to the postscript of the first edition, and although he withdrew it
from subsequent editions he could hardly have thought thereafter
that the authorship was a secret. Furthermore he mentioned five
members of his family by name and as such in his footnotes and
had his own picture engraved on the title page from the third
edition on. He even had it changed, when age had changed him,
so that the resemblance would be closer.

Such "anonymity" can hardly be regarded as a true desire for
privacy; it seems, rather, a form of vanity that desires the glory
of fame *and* the glory of self-effacement. A hidden boast, a secret

vaunt, was dear to his heart. He loved to involve himself in little obscurities, to lie hidden in a cocoon woven of minute mystifications. Nothing was too trifling to serve as a lurking hole. It was his custom, for instance, to add three *r*'s in the form of an inverted pyramid (ᵣʳ) under his signature in the books in his library, a peculiarity that had often been noted and commented upon, but which had to wait until 1912 for elucidation. In that year P. Henderson Aitken, when examining Burton's books in Christ Church library, found in one volume a rough pen and ink sketch of a fesse between two dogs' heads above and one below, with the following explanatory distich in Burton's handwriting:

> Trina canum capita in cyano radiantia scuto
> Sunt gentiliciis symbola clara meis.

Now, the heraldic charge for the Burtons of Lindley, Leicestershire, bore "Arg., a fesse between three talbots heads erased or." And if we recall, as Mr. Aitken reminds us, that the letter *r* is the "litera canina" of the rhetoricians Persius and Donatus, whom Burton frequently quotes, and if, furthermore, we bear in mind the three *r*'s in Burton's own name, we see, with the help of his distich, how, under the double concealment of a cryptographic pun he was able every time he signed his name to boast of his noble descent, despite the fact that he professed to be utterly indifferent to such matters.[15]

This trifle epitomizes one of the patterns of his personality—pride disguised as humility, anonymity industriously providing a clew to its own identification. That this particular secret was so dark that it remained unsuspected for three hundred years, and was only then solved by the merest chance, would most likely have pleased him greatly, could he have known of it.

Much of the time Burton seems to be extremely candid with his reader. He indulges in personal recollections. He gives names and dates and places. He boldly commits himself to the most emphatic opinions. And yet, despite all this, one lays down the book with a feeling that its author is elusive, noncommittal, and evasive. His interminable quotations serve as a screen. By speaking so much through other men's mouths and, particularly, by quoting opinions from both sides of any controversy, he often avoids the responsibility of taking a stand. He has an exasperating trick of half confessing certain sentiments and then as uncertainly disavowing them. His motto, " 'Tis all mine, and none mine," was not lightly chosen. He advances a mass of what one assumes is meant to be convincing testimony, only to dismiss it all in the end as so much rubbish, the "ravings of dizzards." He loves to balance opposing statements in perfect counterpoise, leaving the issue unsettled. His attacks, as Keats has said, are "snarl and countersnarl."

His frustrations show on almost every page. "The *Anatomy* is not a bitter book, but it contains the harvest of much bitterness." [16] He dilates upon the pleasures which he felt had been denied him and is contemptuous of those he has. "I long," he says repeatedly, "but I may not have."

He felt not only his own wasted opportunities but also those of the whole world. The painful, shrunken thing that life was, compared to the vigorous and glorious thing it might be, haunted him. He mourns with genuine feeling over the countless millions of every generation who have faded and died with their potentialities unrealized, their talents atrophied, and their love denied.

Among his private frustrations none is more deeply resented than the celibacy which was then required of fellows. It is "abominable, impious, adulterous and sacrilegious," contrary to the laws of God and man's own best wisdom. It may not have been as great a deprivation as he chose to regard it, but he saw himself as inherently a man of action, and all men of action, he was firmly convinced, had been mighty "doers" in the service of Venus. He will not openly claim any such achievement for himself, but he would not be sorry to have the reader claim it for him. "I have

[16] Middleton Murry, "Burton's Anatomy," in his *Countries of the Mind*, First Series, p. 41.

a tincture," he confesses, with mysterious boldness; "for why should I lie, dissemble or excuse it, yet I'm a man, &c. not altogether inexpert in this subject." [17]

He delights to be amorous in a manly way, to "season a surly discourse" with love matters. He is susceptible, he admits; he is "mightily detained and allured" by the grace and comeliness of women. Merely "to meet or see a fair maid pass by" expels his grief and procures pleasure. With what delight he rolls their sweet names alliteratively on his tongue: "modest Matilda, pretty pleasing Peg, sweet singing Susan, mincing merry Moll, dainty dancing Doll, neat Nancy, jolly Joan, nimble Nell, kissing Kate, bouncing Bess with black eyes, fair Phyllis with fine white hands, fiddling Frances, tall Tib, slender Sib, &c." [18]

He loves to pose as a connoisseur; he is no novice to be taken in by fine linen, a painted face, and a feather in the hat, but a man of the world who knows enough to look for "true color, a solid body and plenty of juice." Love, that's the thing, he cries with gusto; all else is dross! He heartily commends great men who have married for love alone. " 'Twas nobly done of Theodosius to make Eudocia his wife." Most princely was it of Psammetichus, the king of Egypt, to marry Rhodope solely for her beauty. "Great Alexander married Roxane, a poor man's child, only for her person. 'Twas well done of Alexander, and heroically done, I admire him for it." [19]

Yet amid these dainty delights there are ugly smears of misogyny. This lusty smacking of the lips is interspersed with what comes suspiciously close to retchings. Women are "bad by nature and lightly given all." Left to themselves they "think ill . . . for they have no other business to trouble their heads with." To Jacobus de Voragine's "twelve motives to mitigate the miseries of marriage" he is quick to oppose a sneering "Antiparody." [20]

He dwells with morbid fascination upon the "dirtiness" of women, quoting with evident relish the more loathsome passages of the church fathers on the subject. The secret repulsiveness un-

[17] *Anatomy*, p. 762.   [18] *Ibid.*, p. 784.   [19] *Ibid.*, p. 673.   [20] *Ibid.*, p. 817.

derlying their fair-seeming exteriors is ever in his mind. He can't leave it alone, but keeps coming back to it with insistent prurience, gloating over the details of certain physiological processes, which he seems to regard as infinitely more disgusting in women than in men.

His remedy for love is to have the lover see his beloved as she really is. The illusions of men in love fill him with boisterous derision.

Every Lover admires his Mistress [he says], though she be very deformed of herself, ill-favoured, wrinkled, pimpled, pale, red, yellow, tanned, tallow-faced, have a swollen Juggler's platter-face, or a thin, lean, chitty-face, have clouds in her face, be crooked, dry, bald, goggle-ey'd, blear-ey'd, or with staring eyes, she looks like a squis'd cat, hold her head still [continually] awry, heavy, dull, hollow-eyed, black or yellow about the eyes, or squint-eyed, sparrow-mouthed, Persean hook-nosed, have a sharp Fox nose, a red nose, China flat great nose, snub-nose with wide nostrils, a nose like a promontory, gubber-tushed, rotten teeth, black, uneven, brown teeth, beetle-browed, a Witch's beard, her breath stink all over the room, her nose drop winter and summer, with a Bavarian poke under her chin, a sharp chin, lave eared, with a long crane's neck, which stands awry too, with hanging breasts, her dugs like two double jugs, or else no dugs, in the other extreme, bloody-faln [chilblained] fingers, she have filthy long unpared nails, scabbed hands or wrists, a tanned skin, a rotten carkass, crooked back, she stoops, is lame, splay-footed, as slender in the middle as a Cow in the waist, gouty legs, her ankles hang over her shoes, her feet stink, she breeds lice, a mere changeling, a very monster, an auf [oaf, or elf], imperfect, her whole complexion savours, an harsh voice, incondite gesture, vile gait, a vast virago, or an ugly Tit, a slug, a fat fustilugs, a truss, a long lean rawbone, a skeleton . . . whom thou couldest not fancy for a world, but hatest, loathest . . . the very antidote of love to another man, a dowdy, a slut, a scold, a nasty, rank, rammy, filthy, beastly quean, dishonest [unchaste] peradventure, obscene, base, beggarly, rude, foolish, untaught, peevish. . . . [Yet] if he love her once, he admires her for all this, he takes no notice of any such errors, or imperfections of body or mind. . . . He had rather have her than any woman in the world. If he were a King, she alone should be his Queen, his Empress. O that he had but the wealth and treasure of both the Indies to endow her with.[21]

There are many other ways and places in the course of the *Anatomy* in which Burton unconsciously reveals himself—if that may be termed unconscious which he himself freely admits: "I have laid myself open (I know it) in this treatise," he confesses, "turned mine inside outward." [22] His humor, for instance, perhaps the dominating feature of the book, is primarily aggressive. No writer has ever brought together more, or more ingenious, terms of abuse. Like Rabelais, he loved to catalogue vituperation, to pile scurrility upon scurrility. But more often his attack is sly and hidden, giving innocent-seeming sentences an unexpected, puckish twist. He is blandly impudent, saying terrible things under an assumed ignorance of their true significance. His wit loves to lurk in double meanings; it retreats into ambiguities and dissolves into nonsense.

Much of his aggression is directed against the reader, as though he secretly despised those who would waste their time on him. Perhaps the incredible amount of Latin that he uses and the myriads of recondite and awful-sounding authors that he quotes constitute, also, a form of attack. Is his elaborate pedantry a part of himself or a mask from behind which he is laughing at us? Does he not possibly hope to puzzle the reader, to make him feel ignorant and uneasy? Or perhaps—most delicious wound of all! —to lead him into a ludicrous assent to learning that he does not actually understand?

So some critics have insisted and in their exasperation have played into his hands by angrily denying that his authorities and quotations were genuine. The whole thing, they have maintained, is a vast practical joke, but Burton was not the man to have flat-

---

[21] *Ibid.*, pp. 737–738. This dreadful passage, by the way, was greatly admired by Keats, who also felt that a cruel fate had denied him the love of women. He copied it out entire into a letter that he wrote to his brother George, and added: "There's a dose for you. Fire!! I would give my favourite leg to have written this . . ." See *The Complete Works of John Keats*, ed. by H. Buxton Forman, Glasgow, 1901 (reprinted 1923), V, 106.

[22] *Anatomy*, p. 22.

tered the ignorant by any joke that they could comprehend. There are tricks a-plenty, but none so stupid as merely making up Latin quotations. The dullest reader in the seventeenth century would hardly have regarded *that* as whimsical.

Just how involved some of his humor is, is shown in the odd way in which, in some of his translation, he mixes pedantry and colloquialisms. To translate, as he does, *veritas odium parit* as "Verjuice and oatmeal is good for a parrot" is, obviously, a piece of sheer horseplay, a wild caper intended to make the learned laugh and to puzzle the pompous. It was not assumed for a moment that anyone would be misled; everyone who could then read knew that much Latin. The humor lay in the absurdity, the preposterousness of it. It was a piece of gross impudence.

But his lighter changes, his breezy and slangy renditions of the most solemn passages, are not so easy to understand. Sometimes he is just being gay, as in his references to "Mr. Aristotle" and "Uncle Pliny." Or he is being pert, as when he concludes an interminable list of moral maxims by telling the reader that if he desires more he will find them "in Isocrates, Seneca, Plutarch, Epictetus, &c., and for defect, consult with cheese trenchers and painted cloths." That is, he says, if the reader lacks the works of these authors or, possibly, the ability to read them, he can find the same sort of cheap wisdom in the cheap imitations of tapestry which were then used by the poor or in the mottoes carved around the edges of wooden dishes.

"If you can tell how, you may sing this to the tune a sowgelder blows," he jauntily directs the reader in a footnote to some doggerel lines of his own composing.

Usually, however, he is more subtle, preferring to tease the reader by supporting his simplest thought with some abstruse quotation fetched from the far end of all knowledge, but so mistranslated in the carriage that its meaning is ultimately entirely his own.

It is not clear whether his ostentation of learning is a cover for his aggressiveness or a genuine intellectual trait which is continually clashing with and being deflected by his aggressiveness. The latter seems more likely. The effect of a learned quotation is again and again destroyed by some ludicrous colloquialism in its translation. The reader, particularly the solemn simpleton, is, plainly, meant to be confused. Such a style must have exasperated his learned associates in the university, who no doubt prided themselves on the *exclusion* of the vernacular from their writings—and their exasperation must have been a source of great pleasure to Burton.

Now all these characteristics—the resentments, the continual self-depreciation, the discontent, the aggressiveness, the mingled gaiety and depression—fit into a psychological pattern which the known facts of his life do not at least contradict, and it is a pattern which has a considerable bearing on his own psychiatric theories and interpretations.

Denied love in his childhood, whether actually or in fantasy, he was ever after, in his own mind, rejected, discriminated against, and cut off from the opportunities and pleasures which were permitted to others. This attitude of mind gave him a sympathetic insight into the minds of other such people; he knew their pains, their fears, and the inner consequences of their frustrations. As he himself said, he got much of his knowledge from "melancholizing."

But he felt that his fears, his feeling of insecurity in a loveless world, had forced him into a bad bargain. He could have been so much more than a college don if fate had not tricked him. And he never ceased to resent that fact, so that resentment became almost his dominant mood. He remained timid, and consequently his resentment does not dare to show itself too openly; it is cloaked in ambiguity, muffled in disarming absurdity, and strikes obliquely, anonymously, or under the protection of a quotation. But it is always there. It adds greatly to the pungency of his style, but it imposes certain limitations on his mind.

The Book

THE/Anatomy of/Melancholy,/*what it is.*/With all the Kindes,/ Cavses, Symptomes, Prog-/*nostickes, and seve-/rall cvres of it.*/In Three Maine Partitions/with their seuerall Sections, Mem-/bers, and Subsec-/tions./*Philosophically, Medici-/nally, historically, ope-/ned and cvt vp.*/By/Democritus *Iunior.*/ With a Satyricall Preface, conducing to/*the following Discourse.*/Macrob./Omne meum, Nihil meum./*At Oxford,*/Printed by Iohn Lichfield and Iames/Short, for Henry Cripps./*Anno Dom.* 1621

So ran the title page of the first edition.

"Anatomy" in the sense of an "analysis" had become a common term in book titles ever since Stubbes's *Anatomie of Abuses,* so that its use, together with the promise of "a Satyricall Preface," seemed to offer the prospective purchaser one of those castigations of the age of which that particular age was so fond. Burton himself was not fully pleased with the title, which may well have been urged upon him by the bookseller. It is a "phantastical title," he says, designed to catch the eye of "silly passengers . . . that will not look at a judicious piece."

The eye of the passenger, once caught, would have found the volume to be composed of a long satirical introduction, a detailed consideration of the symptoms, causes, and treatment of melancholy, and three long digressions—one on anatomy, one on "air rectified," and one on the nature of supernatural beings.

The introduction, consisting largely of a survey of the vices and follies of the age, was vigorous enough in its attack to please the most censorious, and the silliest passenger that ever passed a bookstall would have found nothing to desire in the digression on devils. But the serious part of the work might well have puzzled those who bought books wholly on the strength of their "phantastical titles," though, fortunately for such, it was so buried in anecdotes and quotations, so diffused and so diluted with asides and not-entirely-relevant illustrations, that they may have missed it altogether. The intelligent, earnest reader, however, who burrowed through all this, would have found himself amply repaid for his trouble.

The treatise itself is divided into three main partitions, and each of these is divided into sections, members, and subsections. Before each partition there is a synopsis. The first partition deals with the causes, symptoms, and prognostics of melancholy. The second is devoted to its cure. The third is concerned with love melancholy and religious melancholy.

Though the tone of the book is often gay, even boisterous at times, its purpose is serious. That this has not always been recognized cannot be blamed on Burton, for he states it plainly enough:

> my purpose & endeavour is, in the following discourse [he says] to anatomize this humour of melancholy, through all his parts and species, as it is an habit, or an ordinary disease, and that philosophically, medicinally, to shew the causes, symptoms, and several [individual, particular] cures of it, that it may be the better avoided; moved thereunto for the generality of it, and to do good, it being a disease so frequent . . . as few there are that feel not the smart of it.[1]

Those critics who have been inclined to regard the *Anatomy* as a practical joke have found their strongest evidence in the incredible complexity, the endless divisions and subdivisions, of the synopses which precede each partition. And, certainly, they are enough to exhaust the greatest patience. "An enormous labyrinthine joke," cries one baffled critic; "the grossest fooling." [2]

But nothing could be farther from the truth; as a matter of fact, they offer conclusive proof of Burton's seriousness. For, however strange they may seem to us, these elaborate synopses were

[1] *Anatomy*, p. 101.
[2] Brown, "Robert Burton (Causerie)," *New Review*, XIII (1895), 258–259.

then the regular procedure in all medical treatises, and his use of them shows that he thought, at least, that he was writing a medical work.

Actually a few minutes' study is sufficient to dispel the difficulties offered by their unusual form, and they appear for what they are, excellent summaries. Much of their seeming absurdity is due to the outworn physical and metaphysical concepts upon which the book is based. When, for instance, we find God and sin listed as direct causes of disease, or when we find the internal organs of the body classified as "noble" and "ignoble," it is plain that the writer is thinking within concepts that have since been eliminated from medical theory.

But it would be a mistake to dismiss him, solely because of this, as a buffoon. It does, indeed, require, it must be confessed, a high degree of a special sort of tolerance to continue reading, with any expectation of being enlightened, a medical work which groups "baldness, falling of hair, dandruff and lice" as diseases "belonging properly to the brain." [3] But, nonetheless, just such a tolerance is required whenever we seek to evaluate the thought of a past generation. To reject an entire work because of a difference in the basis of classifications is to be intellectually provincial. The pre-Linnaean world seems an extraordinary place to us, but the men who thought in it were not necessarily fools. Locke, for instance, classifies seals and mermaids as links between aquatic and terrestrial animals and flying fish as links between fish and birds. Still higher up the scale he places angels.[4] But the *Essay concerning Human Understanding*, in which these astonishing categories occur, remains, nonetheless, a significant contribution to psychology.

So when Burton adopts the Hippocratic division of the body into "parts containing" and "parts contained" we know, with the wisdom of hindsight, that he is enmeshed in a concept that will severely limit his anatomical thinking. But it does not in any way

[3] *Anatomy*, p. 120.
[4] John Locke, *An Essay concerning Human Understanding*, Book III, chap. vi, sec. 12.

invalidate his observations. The concept of "mind" and "body" which dominates almost all lay thinking today is, really, just as absurd. Yet many men have made valuable additions to knowledge within its limitations. Perhaps the concept of any organ of the body as an entity, or even the concept of the body itself as an entity, is equally fallacious.

The Anatomy of Melancholy presents many other difficulties. In any edition except that modernized by Paul Jordan-Smith and Floyd Dell the typography alone would daunt all but the most hardened. The archaic spelling, the use of the long "s," and the interchange of "u" and "v" are serious barriers to those who are not specialists in Elizabethan literature. The pages bristle with italics, quotation marks, parentheses, and astrological signs. The margins are crammed with notes in minute type, most of them in Latin and identified by a series of Roman numerals and cabalistic abbreviations, the whole forming so formidable a conglomeration that the inexperienced reader can hardly be blamed for losing heart at the outset. A very little while suffices to remove much of the strangeness, but the first looking into Burton's *Anatomy* remains for most an unforgettable experience.[5]

Worst of all, perhaps, are the quotations. They are incredible. Their number exceeds all belief. It has been estimated that the book contains excerpts from nearly one thousand authors, about half of whom are medical writers, comprising almost every name of consequence in medicine from the fifth century to the seventeenth century. The rest are classical writers, theologians, philosophers, dramatists, historians, satirists, and poets. By any known standard Burton must be regarded as one of the most learned men that ever lived.

And he is proud of it! He makes a parade of his indebtedness, preferring, often, it would seem, to appear learned rather than original. Even where the thought is plainly his own, he will scour antiquity until he finds a passage that will approximate it. "I have

[5] Pages 33–34 contain a paragraph from the 6th edition of *The Anatomy of Melancholy* instead of from the modernized edition, from which all other quotations in this book are drawn; but the difficulties of the older type and paper cannot be adequately reproduced here.

laboriously collected this Cento out of divers writers," he states, belittling his own part in the work, "and that without injury, I have wronged no authors, but given every man his own." When two or three—or a dozen, for that matter—have said the same thing, he will gladly quote them all.

And what authorities they are! The reader starts back in awe from Frambesarius, Strozzius Cicogna, Baptista Codronchus, Frismelica, Wolfongus Hider, Pamphilus Hirelacus, Laelius à Fonte Eugubinus, and a hundred more like-sounding names. Infallibility hedges them about with syllables through which skepticism dares but peep. Who so bold as to question Jodocus Damhoderius or Fromundus of Louvain? What man so rash as to contradict Sozomenus, Galgerandus of Mantua, or "that Clazomenian Hermotimus"? [6]

Those who maintain that the *Anatomy* is a practical joke have sought to remove the uneasiness of their ignorance by insisting that these intellectual dinosaurs never existed outside Burton's figmentitious fancy. But this is not true. They are, or were, real men and did write huge tomes under those tremendous names. At least one supposes they wrote huge tomes; nothing less than folios could have been commensurate with their dignity. But even if they wrote only little pocket books, they did exist and did write. Scholarship—assisted in no small part by Burton's own library— has laboriously traced them to their lairs in the idle deserts and vast antres of forgotten thought.

The grandeur of their names is in a large part due to the medieval custom of latinizing names and often adding the place of residence or birth. Pomponatius of Padua, for instance, who decorates so many passages in the *Anatomy*, is still read, or at least

[6] Just to show that this has by no means exhausted the list, here are a dozen more: Fulgosus, Lampsacus, Aloysius Cadamustus, Papirius Massovius, Didacus Astunica, Panormitan, Nigidius Figulus, Sigismundus Scheretzius, Buxtorfius, Calcagninus, Nicephorus Gregoras, and Sextus ab Heminga. Swift, Sterne, Lamb, and, more recently, Anatole France have all added a touch of grave whimsicality to their works by introducing the most recondite authorities, the first three in obvious parody of Burton. That their intent is plainly humorous may, in some measure, account for the misinterpretation of Burton's motive.

quoted, by theologians under the less horrendus name Pomponazzi.

Doctors, particularly, used to translate their names into Latin in order to be impressive. "Montanus," for instance, was more likely to awe a patient than "Dr. Hill." And the mystery that surrounds Quercetan, Villanovus, Camerarius, and Sacrobosco is decidedly lessened in their Englished equivalents—Drs. Oak, Newton, Chambers, and Holywood.

That so many of these strange names appear in the *Anatomy* is to some extent due to what has been called the texture of a forgotten mode of thought, though there be no doubt that Burton carried the fashion into idiosyncrasy. The trick that he did so well became a habit, and the habit an obsession. He brings up masses of testimony to support what is self-evident, and the more recondite the authority, the happier he is. That the map of the world, for example, has a fancied resemblance to a fool's head is plainly a Burtonian conceit; yet how pleased he is to be able to tell us that Epichthonius Cosmopolites had entertained the same idea. One hardly knows whether the authority was introduced for the sake of the reference or the reference for the sake of the authority.

He does not perceive or does not care that many of his authorities are secondary. He will quote an original source and proceed to support it by a derivative. Thus he gives us Matthiolus's account of a parish priest who was cured of melancholy after twelve grains of stibium had purged him (as well it might!) of "a deal of black choler, like little gobbets of flesh," and adds that the story must be true because Sckenkius relates the same incident "word for word." Whereas to a modern scholar the "word for word" would suggest that one of the accounts was derivative or that they had a common source.

It would be a mistake, however, to regard the *Anatomy* as nothing more than a mosaic of borrowings. There is certainly too much quoting to suit our taste, but, as Dr. Johnson observed, "there is great spirit and power in what Burton says when he writes from his own mind."

And it is worth repeating that he is often writing from his own mind when he is quoting. He thought in books. He expressed himself in other men's words; but it was *himself* that he expressed. His authorities were the bricks with which he built, and it would be as unreasonable to dismiss him from consideration because he draws most of his clinical evidence from others as it would be to dismiss a modern psychiatrist because he does not make up his case histories. Books were his experience, the only wide experience that his retired life afforded; they were his windows to the world of the past and the present.

It must be confessed that he looked through them rather uncritically. He dearly loved the quaint, the out of the way, the extraordinary, and even when he can't believe he is unwilling to deny. He has only the dubious authority of "Florentius his Georgicks" for the statement that palm trees fall in love and are "marvellously affected" when the wind brings them the smell of each other, but it is plain that he would like to believe it. He tries to be impartial concerning the sovereign virtues of precious stones, but all the evidence he presents is favorable. He seems to have no doubt whatever that a corpse will bleed "when the murderer is brought before it" and challenges atheists to account for this by any means other than the hand of providence.

He hesitates to assent to the extraordinary, but he loves to hover in the background and murmur, "You never can tell!"

Of course he had to thread his way through some remarkable material. Seventeenth-century medicine (or, rather, sixteenth-century, for the *Anatomy* was written too early in the seventeenth century to benefit by anything but the previous century's learning) was an amalgam of superstition and magic with commonsense observations. It incorporated old wives' tales and folklore with remedies tested in practice, and seemed not to distinguish the one from the other. The great physicians were still the ancients and their Arabic successors, whose teaching, erroneous in many respects, had been vitiated by false translations, textual corruptions, and the embroideries of generations of charlatans. Burton had neither the training nor the knowledge that would have been required to sift this mass and separate the false from the true. But then, nor had anyone else in his day.

Aside from the burden of quotations the *Anatomy* is brisk and energetic. Burton asserts that it has no style at all, that he wrote it "standing on one leg," with as small deliberation as he spoke. It is "a rhapsody of rags," he says cheerfully, written in a "Dorick dialect" and "confusedly tumbled out, without art, invention, judgment, wit [or] learning." He anticipates every possible stricture: it is "harsh, raw, crude, phantastical, absurd, indolent, indiscreet, ill-composed, indigested, vain, scurrile, idle, dull and dry." He says he is merely "a loose, plain, rude writer," who calls a spade a spade and follows nothing but the dictates of his shifting moods.

'Tis not my study or intent [he confesses, or, rather, boasts] to compose neatly . . . but to express myself readily & plainly as it happens. So that as a River runs, sometimes precipitate and swift, then dull and slow; now direct, then winding; now deep, then shallow; now muddy, then clear; now broad, then narrow; doth my style flow: now serious, then light; now comical, then satirical; now more elaborate, then remiss, as the present subject required, or as at that time I was affected.[7]

His virtue is gusto. His excited mind overleaps the trammels of syntax and soars into catalogues of abuse or rapture. A dozen synonyms suddenly spout like geysers from the middle of a sentence, and his latinity seems to increase the violence rather than to impede the progress of his expression, like boulders in the current of a mountain stream.

A turbulent haste hurries his words along. But, rapidly as they move, his mind seems ever to be ahead of them, impatiently tugging. Half of his sentences stop short, once their meaning has been indicated, and end with a sort of splutter or fizz in an "&c.," probably the most-used piece of type in the book. He gets swept along in the flow of his own thoughts, flailing about him mightily, but unable to stop or turn aside until the flood has spent its force. Learned polysyllables and slang swirl merrily together. Words such as "stramineous," "obtretaction," "calamistrate," "amphibological," and "terriculaments" stud every page, joined with dia-

---

[7] *Anatomy*, p. 25; see also pp. 974–975. Earlier quotations in this paragraph are from pp. 974, 20, 24–25.

lect and colloquialisms such as "freckons," "livor," "lask," "mormoluches," "hone [yearn]," "cample," "pintle," and "fuseled." As far as his vocabulary goes there is no affectation of either erudition or simplicity; he is as willing to use one set of words as another or to compound them into such phrases as "circumforanean rogues," "facete companions," or "turgent titles." A great deal of the flavor of his style derives from these unexpected juxtapositions.

He abounds with homely vigor: doctors are "purse milkers" and "piss prophets"; lawyers are "gowned vultures"; students are poor things who "turn pallid over mere paper" and, for the most part, "bring nothing to their degree but the desire to take it." Old men will dance, he says scornfully, "who have more toes than teeth." Proselyting usually begins with "collapsed ladies." He dismisses purgatory and limbo as "all that subterranean Geography."

He delights in invective. He loves to give his aggressiveness free rein and to gallop roughshod, helter-skelter, over all that annoys him. The excesses of sexual desire, for instance, seemed to have a fascination of repulsion for him. It is his favorite subject for castigation.

Of womens unnatural,[h] unsatiable lust [he says], what Country, what Village doth not complain? Mother and daughter sometimes dote on the same man, father and son, master and servant on one woman.
—*Sed amor, sed in effrenata libido,*
   Quid castum in terris intentatumq; reliquit?
What breach of vows and oaths, fury, dotage, madness, might I reckon up? Yet this is more tolerable in youth, and such as are still in their hot blood; but for an old fool to dote, to see an old leacher, what more odious, what can be more absurd? and yet what so common? Who so furious?
† *Amare ea ætate si occiperint, multo insaniunt acriùs.*
Some dote then more then ever they did in their youth. How many decrepit, hoary, harsh,

[h] *De Mulierum in exhausta libidine luxuq; insatiabili omnes æque regiones conqueri posse existimo Steph.*

† *Plautus.*

writhen, bursten-bellied, crooked, toothless, bald, blear-eyed, impotent, rotten, old men shall you see flickering still in every place? One gets him a young wife, another a Curtisan, and when he can scarce lift his leg over a sill, and hath one foot already in *Charons* boat, when he hath the trembling in his joynts, the gout in his feet; a perpetual rhume in his head, *a continuate cough,** his sight fails him, thick of hearing, his breath stinks,* all his moisture is dried up and gone, may not spit from him; a very child again, that cannot dress himself, or cut his own meat, yet he will be dreaming of, and honing after wenches, what can be more unseemly? Worse it is in women then in men, when she is † *ætate declivis, diu vidua, mater olim, parum decorè matrimonium sequi videtur,* an old widdow, a mother so long since († in *Plinies* opinion) she doth very unseemly seek to marry, yet whilst she is [i] so old a crone, a beldame, she can neither see, nor hear, go nor stand, a meer [k] Karcass, a witch, and scarce feel; she catterwauls, and must have a stallion, a Champion, she must and will marry again, and betroth her self to some yong man,[l] that hates to look on [her], but for her goods; abhors the sight of her, to the prejudice of her good name, her own undoing, grief of friends, and ruin of her children.[8]

* Oculi caligant aures graviter audiunt, capilli fluunt, cutis avescit, flatus olet, tussis, &c. Cyprian.

† Lib. 8. Epist. Ruffinus.
[i] Hiatq; turpis inter aridas nates podex.
[k]. Cadaverosa adeo ut ab inferis reversa videri possit vult adhuc catullire.
[l]. Nam & matrimoniis est despectum senium.
Æneas Silvius

His metaphors are racy and earthy, sharply arresting. There is no pedantry in such phrases as "cheaper than seaweed," "as keen as a new-ground hatchet," and "land-leaping Jesuits." To attempt to reform some people, he says, is but "washing a mudbrick." Venus was "as common as a barber's chair." Applause fattens men "as frost doth conies." "As much pity is to be taken of a woman weeping as of a goose going barefoot." An old man who marries a young wife builds a mill to grind one peck of corn. He who guards his wealth and neglects his children "is more careful of his

[8] *Anatomy*, 6th ed., London, 1652, p. 445. This one paragraph is copied from Burton's text instead of the modernized edition.

shoes than of his feet." Some women would be "as well pleased with one eye as one man." The lover thinks his mistress the most beautiful creature on earth, though to other men she looks "like a merd in a lanthorn." And so forth.

It is the abundance of such phrases that gives the *Anatomy* so much space in dictionaries of quotations. For if he quotes freely, he is also freely quoted: "Sickness is the mother of modesty," "Frost and fraud come to foul ends," "What can't be cured must be endured," and a score of other aphorisms that have passed into common use achieved their best-known forms under his hand.

One characteristic of his style is so striking that it could serve as his hallmark. He has a habit of interrupting himself to comment on, illustrate, or exclaim over some statement that he has just made. He will dramatize his own generalities or suddenly answer a question which he assumes some reader to have asked. It is as though he were looking over his own shoulder as he wrote, amazed, delighted, and even exasperated, at times, by his own narrative. For example, in a celebrated passage on the beauty of women which he is translating from St. Chrysostom there is a reference to "a fair and beautiful person." To which Burton immediately, in parentheses, adds a sort of smacking of the lips: "(a brave Bonaroba, or well-dress'd woman, a beautiful Donna who'd make your mouth water, a merry girl and one not hard to love)." [9] Or, to give another instance, in the course of quoting various authorities pro and con on the then much-debated question of the motion of the earth he becomes excited at the fury of the disputants and interjects "sound Drums and Trumpets" in parentheses. [10]

Much of the time he appears to be musing to himself, to be more in the act of composing than engaged in setting down organized thoughts. He will repeat an idea in several different phrases, as though seeking for the most suitable expression. "I had rather repeat words ten times," he confesses innocently, "than omit anything."

[9] *Anatomy*, p. 785.
[10] *Ibid.*, p. 427; for other instances see pp. 242, 326, 536, 551, 837, 915.

His style reflects his tangential mind. An idea suggests an author who, in turn, suggests another idea, and this second idea may have to be qualified, affirmed, or contradicted by a second author who, in his turn, will suggest a third idea, and so forth. And all of these will be jumbled into a single paragraph or even a single sentence. Clause is grooved into clause like a nest of Chinese boxes. The bewildered reader sometimes emerges from these syntactical labyrinths in complete confusion, unable to see any relevance whatever in the final clauses. But if he will go back and make a mental diagram as he reads, he will discover that the parts are properly related and that the disparate last clause is the logical conclusion of the simple statement which in the tenth line back led him into the maze.

An example will serve better than any description. In his address to the reader Burton promises that he will make amends for thus meddling with medicine by writing another work later in his true capacity as a divine. He compares himself to one of the medieval bishops of Lincoln, who built six castles and then sought to allay public resentment of such unclerical grandeur by building six religious edifices. This story he had read in Camden's *Britannia*, but he is skeptical of it, because the same thing is told in the same words by Nubrigensis concerning Roger of Salisbury, who, in King Stephen's reign, built the castles of Sherborne and Devizes. And all of this—his own statement, comparisons, authorities, quotations, and qualifications—is built into one sentence! Here it is:

If these reasons do not satisfy thee, Good Reader, as Alexander Munificus, that bountiful Prelate sometime Bishop of Lincoln, when he had built six Castles, to take away the envy of his work, saith Mr. Camden, (which very words Nubrigensis hath of Roger the rich Bishop of Salisbury, who in King Stephen's time built Sherborne Castle, and that of Devizes) to divert the scandal or imputation which might be thence inferred, built so many Religious Houses; if this my discourse be over medicinal, or savour too much of humanity, I promise thee that I will hereafter make thee amends in some treatise of divinity.[11]

One of the most difficult features of the book to a modern reader is the tremendous amount of Latin it contains. Perhaps a

[11] *Ibid.*, p. 30.

fifth of the entire volume is in Latin, and in an age when a reading knowledge of that language cannot be taken for granted, not even among the educated, that fact alone is enough to make the book unreadable. It may have been the *Anatomy* that led Sir Thomas Browne to complain that if certain writers persisted in their courses we should have to learn Latin in order to read English.

The incredible amount of Latin in the *Anatomy* represents, in a way, a compromise. Burton wanted to write the whole thing in Latin; "It was not mine intent," he says roundly, "to prostitute my muse in English, or to divulge the secrets of Minerva." But the "mercenary stationers" wouldn't look at a book written in Latin, though they would publish *any*thing in English, he adds bitterly, and "pound out pamphlets on the leaves of which even a poverty-stricken monkey would not wipe."

Still, he made as little concession to the mercenary stationers as any man could who claimed to be writing in English. Sometimes he uses Latin for professional privacy—as in his description of sexual perversions, to which he adds a special injunction: "Good master Schoolmaster, do not English this." He put his prescriptions into Latin, as he avows, so that the unlearned reader might not be tempted to practice upon himself. And with filial respect (possibly in obedience to Leviticus 18:7) he hides his suggestions for reforming the university under the same discreet veil.

He translates a great many of his quotations, most of them, in fact, in the sentences immediately ensuing, but the cursory reader may be excused if he does not always perceive this, for the translations are often so free that they can hardly be called paraphrases. "The matter is theirs most part," he explains, "yet it appears as something different from what 'tis taken from." As "nature doth with the aliment of our bodies, incorporate, digest, assimilate," so he did with his authors. He compares himself to a housewife who "out of divers fleeces weaves one piece of cloth." The basic stuff of the book is his authors', but the final shape and pattern is his.

And so we find such renditions as "hang him that hath no money" for *absque argento omnia vana* and "he is a meer hog that rejects any man for his poverty" for *Est porcus ille qui sacerdotem ex amplitudine redituum sordide demetitur.* Sometimes a quotation is given a fillip by the insertion of an extra word, as "The race is not to the swift, nor the battle to the strong, but as the wise man said, chance, and sometimes a ridiculous chance."

The quaint energy of his style contributed greatly, no doubt, to the success of his book, but a measure of its success was unquestionably due to the extraordinary range of his interests. The seventeenth century loved erudition, and Burton was their man. Since his subject was the human mind, he felt that nothing was alien that had ever concerned the human mind or that the human mind had ever been concerned with. Which is to say that nothing whatever was outside his plan; everything was grist that came to his mill—poetry, medicine, psychology, philosophy, philology, history, art, theology, diet, climatology, travel, politics, folklore, astrology—anything and everything.

De Quincey boasted that he alone had circumnavigated literature, but that was the arrogance of a romantic; Burton had probably sailed stranger seas than De Quincey dreamed of, and from his sweeping journeys into the literature of antiquity and the Middle Ages he brought back many a rare and curious thing to attest the vagaries of the mind, the preposterousness of human conduct, and the age and strength of custom. From the *Anatomy* we learn, among other things, that "Persian Kings hawk after Butterflies with sparrows," that "Domitian the Emperor was much delighted with catching flies," and that the Romans regarded a wife's smearing her husband's face with lipstick as one of the inescapable evils of marriage.[12]

Much of the book's lore is of a most doubtful factual value, but it is fascinating all the same. What were "those two green children which Nubrigensis speaks of in his time that fell from Heaven"? What was Burgravius's mysterious "Lamp of Life and Index of Death," and what was the secret of his skill in appeasing ghosts with strange perfumes? And did "Mr. Carew of Anthony" actually see those musical whales which he "saith . . . will come

[12] *Ibid.,* pp. 442, 448, 863.

and shew themselves dancing at the sound of a trumpet"? [13]

Burton is often incredulous, but the weird and wonderful had a powerful attraction for him, and he puts it all down, without claiming our credence, simply for his own delight—and ours. That a "Thessalian Thero . . . bit off his own thumb, to make his Corrival do as much" is possible, and if it were attempted it is well to have it recorded. It is interesting to know that maids practiced cromnysmantia, "a kind of Divination with Onions laid on the Altar on Christmas Eve," and that huntsmen gave their dogs magic philters to make them love them. That Lapps were averse to baptism because they invariably die "within seven or nine days after" is open to question, but it is curious to know that such a belief existed as a part of the legend of that strange people.[14]

The *Anatomy* is a mine of folklore. In its pages the Old Man of the Mountain makes one of his earliest appearances, and there, for the first time in English, we read that "at Hammel in Saxony, on the 20th of June, 1484, the Devil, in the likeness of a pied piper, carried away 130 children, that were never after seen." [15] In the *Anatomy*, for perhaps the last time with any expectation of credence, appear the dancers of Colewitz. These unhappy young people had been singing and dancing in the churchyard "in the year 1012, at Colewiz, in Saxony, on Christmas Eve," and refused to be quiet when the priest ordered them to. In punishment St. Magnus compelled them to dance day and night without ceasing for a year, until on the next Christmas Eve the priest interceded for them. By Burton's time they had danced their moral lesson through a hundred homilies, and their continuance until so late a date marks them as one of the most vital of myths.[16]

Anthony Wood tells us that by the end of the seventeenth century the *Anatomy* had become recognized as a great storehouse of information, whence "Gentlemen who have lost their time

[13] *Ibid.*, pp. 425, 462, 720, 968–969, 479n.
[14] *Ibid.*, pp. 747, 758, 720, 877.   [15] *Ibid.*, pp. 883, 173.
[16] *Ibid.*, p. 758. "Colewitz" is more often "Colbeck" or "Kolbig." As the Pied Piper is thought by some to be a folk memory of the Children's Crusade, so the dancers are thought to be a folk memory of the medieval dance manias. See J. F. C. Hecker, *The Dancing Mania of the Middle Ages*, New York, 1885, p. 8.

and are put to a push for invention, may furnish themselves with matter for common or scholastical discourse and writing." [17] And certainly they must have found this short cut to learning a primrose path, enriched with curious anecdotes and enlivened with many a "pleasant dotage." There are such interesting cases as that of the deluded gentleman "at Senes in Italy" who retained his urine lest he flood the town, and would, no doubt, have died of uremia had not a crafty physician sounded the fire alarm. There is the ingenious baker of Basle who secretly castrated himself to see if his wife were bearing only his children, and the charmingly chaste Bilia who believed that all men had halitosis because her husband had.[18]

Demonology then gave delusions a wider scope than they now enjoy, and case histories were correspondingly more colorful. Devils entered, left, and manifested their presence inside the demented in remarkable ways, of which the attending physicians left many instructive accounts. Thus:

Cornelius Gemma relates of a young maid, called Katherine Gualter, a cooper's daughter, in the year 1571, that had such strange passions and convulsions, three men could not sometimes hold her; she purged a live eel, which he saw, a foot and a half long, and touched himself, but the eel afterwards vanished; she vomited some 24 pounds of fulsome stuff of all colours twice a day for 14 days; and after that she voided great balls of hair, pieces of wood, pigeon's dung, parchment, goose dung, coals; and after them two pounds of pure blood, and then again coals and stones, of which some had inscriptions, bigger than a walnut, some of them pieces of glass, brass, &c., besides paroxysms of laughing, weeping and ecstasies, &c. And this (he says), I saw with horror. They could do no good on her by physick, but left her to the Clergy. Marcellus Donatus hath such another story of a country fellow, that had four knives in his belly, indented like a saw, every one a span long, with a wreath of hair like a globe, with much baggage of like sort, wonderful to behold. How it should come into his guts, he concludes, could only have been through the artifice and craft of a daemon. Langius hath many relations to this effect, and so hath Christopherus à Vega. Wierus, Sckenkius, Scribonius, all agree that they are done by the subtility

---

[17] Wood, *Athenae Oxonienses*, I, 627.   [18] *Anatomy*, pp. 477, 847, 853.

and illusion of the Devil. If you shall ask a reason of this, 'tis to exercise our patience.[19]

Many of the stories that lend so much charm to the *Anatomy* seem to have been included merely for their own interest or for the amusement they might afford. It is to Burton's pages that Englishmen, ultimately, owe their knowledge that Bishop Hatto was eaten by mice ("which howsoever Serrarius the Jesuit impugns by 22 arguments, Trithemius, Munster, Magdeburgenses, and many others relate for a truth") and of the young man who innocently married a lamia. Less known, but equally pitiable, is an anonymous martyr to rival rectitudes of whom Burton tells, a Jew of Magdeburg who, in the year 1270, had the misfortune to fall down a privy on Saturday. The Jews wouldn't pull him out because it was the Sabbath, the bishop forbade anyone to pull him out on Sunday, and by Monday it was too late.[20]

If Burton's conversation was "very innocent," as Hearne reports, it differed slightly from his writing, for imbedded in the *Anatomy* is many a jest which, as he boasted, would make chaste matrons cry "Pish!" and yet read on. Such as the comment of a worldly wittol of Thrace who on surprising another man in bed with his dowdy and hideous wife "cried out as one amazed: O thou wretch! what necessity brought thee hither?" Or the jape of that resourceful bridegroom who, when his wife was brought to bed of a child two months after the marriage, bought six cradles, with the remark that it would be as well to lay in a year's supply.[21]

He is not always laughing, however. In his wandering through books he came on many an incident that touched his compassion, stories of quiet heroism, unusual suffering, or endurance that caused him to turn aside from his subject for a moment to rescue some act of simple nobility from oblivion by recording it. He was much moved, for example, by Fulgosus's account of an honest country fellow in the Kingdom of Naples who while he was plowing by the seaside saw his wife carried away by Mauritian pirates.

[19] *Ibid.*, pp. 175–176.   [20] *Ibid.*, pp. 945, 648, 921.   [21] *Ibid.* pp. 861, 854.

He ran after in all haste, up to the chin first, and when he could wade
no longer, swam, calling to the Governor of the ship to deliver his
wife, or if he must not have her restored, to let him follow as a pris-
oner, for he was resolved to be a Galley-slave, his drudge, willing to
endure any misery, so that he might but enjoy his dear wife. The
Moors, seeing the man's constancy, and relating the whole matter to
their Governor at Tunis, set them both free, and gave them an honest
pension to maintain themselves during their lives.[22]

With so much humor, pathos, learning, folktales, satire, ribaldry,
and science all mixed together to suit the taste of the age, it is no
wonder that the *Anatomy* had an immediate and great success.
"The first, second, and third editions," as Burton himself tells us,
"were suddenly gone, eagerly read." "Scarcely any book of
philology in our land," says Fuller, "hath in so short a time passed
so many impressions." Five editions appeared in Burton's lifetime and three more within a generation of his death; it became
an indispensable part of every gentleman's library and "a commonplace for filchers."[23]

Yet from the time of the eighth edition (1676) on, its popu-
larity began to decline. Its crabbed wit, involved style, and im-
mense tangle of erudition made it ill-suited to the lucid, if sometimes shallow, rationalism of the eighteenth century. The basic
irrationality of things, the dark mystery of life that had so haunted
and oppressed Burton's generation, was no longer a fashionable
subject of contemplation. Melancholy, which had given more
than one tortured man both life and death, became, at least in the
popular mind, that laughable thing The Spleen, something between bored petulance and hysterics. A long poem that made fun
of it was quite a success, but as for a folio, divided into interminable
ble and forbidding members, sections, and subsections, there simply was no public for it, as the "mercenary stationers" quickly
perceived. By 1733, Hearne mournfully tells us, it was "disregarded," the very best of the old editions could be picked up on
any second-hand bookstall for a shilling.

The eclipse of the book was shared by its author. When the

[22] *Ibid.*, p. 815.   [23] *Reliquiae Hearnianae*, p. 796.

Biographia Britannica appeared in 1747, with its detailed and often garrulous accounts of almost two thousand "eminent Persons who have flourished in Great Britain," Robert Burton was not reckoned among them. Even in the immensely enlarged second edition, thirty years later, he appeared only in a brief footnote.

There were still some readers, of course, but they were the esoteric few. Sterne wrenched a great many of his forced whimsies out of Burton's genuine ones. Johnson, himself, as he often thought, tottering on the edge of madness, read the *Anatomy* avidly; it was the only book, he said, that ever got him out of bed early. But his enthusiasm was not widely shared.

By 1800 a new edition seemed a safe venture, and with its appearance Burton had a second period of fame, a great measure of which, ironically enough, was owed to Lamb's indignant protest against his appearing at all in a modern format. To Lamb, Burton was the essence of quaintness, the "fantastic great old man," whose work was desecrated by being printed in anything but folio. Lamb's outcries brought a host of new readers, but they largely tended to stress his strangeness and obscurity, qualities which he certainly possessed, and even in his own day had done much to conceal his true worth and purpose. Nonetheless, the chatter of the romantic critics aroused attention; *The Anatomy of Melancholy* again became a book which every gentleman was expected to possess, though he was no longer expected to have read it or to embellish his "scholastical discourse" with excerpts from it.

Since 1800 some sixty editions and reprints have appeared. Toward the end of the nineteenth century, particularly, there was a flurry of new editions, and each edition was greeted by a flurry of reviews in which each reviewer sought to distinguish himself as a connoisseur of the quaint.

In addition to this open career, the *Anatomy* has had a peculiar underground existence. Fletcher, Ford, and Milton were indebted to it, as were Addison and, possibly, Swift. Johnson showed its influence in his talk and writing. Two of his most famous strokes of wit, the definition of oats and the comparison of a ship to a prison, are drawn from the *Anatomy*, and although *The Vanity of*

Human Wishes invokes Democritus, its spirit and much of its matter belong to Democritus Junior. Interestingly enough, the *Anatomy* is not quoted in Johnson's *Dictionary;* he said that he had been careful to illustrate the meanings of words by selections drawn only from those authors whose works would not unsettle the religious or moral convictions of the young, and it may have been that he thought Burton too profoundly disturbing.

Sterne stole mercilessly, lifting whole pages from the *Anatomy* almost word for word.[24] That so open a theft passed unchallenged is a clear indication of the extent to which Burton had fallen into oblivion.

Many other writers quarried from the *Anatomy*. Amory's *John Buncle* "is not a plagiary; but if there is such a thing as one book's being inspired by another, then *Buncle* was . . . sired by *The Anatomy*." [25] Lamb deliberately sought to copy Burton's manner. Southey made extensive borrowings. Keats elaborated a hint in the third Partition into *St. Agnes Eve*, and the *Anatomy* furnished him with the idea for *Lamia* and the central thought of the *Ode on Melancholy*.[26] Thackeray and Browning are also indebted to Burton.

But the emphasis of all these borrowings and, indeed, of almost the entire interest in Burton since the end of the seventeenth century has been literary, centering more on his style and digressions than on his central theme. His own diffuseness and eccentricity are partly to blame; many a reader must have gone through the *Anatomy* and emerged with only the vaguest notion of what the central theme, if any, was. But he does not deserve *all* the blame. He says clearly enough that the book was intended to be a serious study of abnormal psychology, and as such it was first accepted.

The late sixteenth and early seventeenth centuries were deeply interested in the aberrations of the mind; the manifestations, causes, and proper treatment of mental disturbances occupied a large place in their thinking and literature, and although many of their theories

[24] Ferriar, *Illustrations of Sterne.*
[25] Jordan-Smith, *Bibliographia Burtoniana*, p. 106.
[26] Dell, "Keats's Debt to Burton," *Bookman*, LXVII (March, 1928), 13–17.

seem to us distorted and inadequate, their observations were acute and honest. They were certainly not inhibited, for example, by the moral queasiness that stultified the popular approach to psychological questions in the late Victorian era. The author of *Hamlet* would, plainly, not have been outraged at the theory of the Oedipus complex. Nor would most of his educated contemporaries; they might not have accepted it as the final word, but they would certainly not have flown into a rage at the mention of it as their great-great-grandchildren did. Havelock Ellis's two great interests, the psychology of sex and the minor Elizabethan and Jacobean dramatists, are not unrelated, for, as Ellis says of John Ford, these writers were "sensitive observers" who "searched intimately and felt with instinctive sympathy the fibres of their hearts." [27]

It is surprising, then, that in the modern renaissance of psychology so little attention has been paid to the work that three hundred years ago, when men were last keenly interested in the nature of the mind, was generally regarded as the definitive work on the subject. There have been one or two faint recognitions of the true nature of the *Anatomy*, but they have not been very widespread or effective. A selection of passages under "psychological" headings was published in the nineteen-twenties, but the selections were few, and no effort was made to arrange them into any system. In 1927 Floyd Dell and Paul Jordan-Smith published what was, perhaps, more important than any interpretation—an edition of the *Anatomy* which, while it did no violence to Burton's thought and little, if any, to his style, was readable. This they accomplished by translating the Latin directly into the text, retaining Burton's own translations wherever they existed, removing italics and many of the capitals, expanding abbreviations, and reducing footnotes to a microscopic minimum. Only those who have worked with *The Anatomy of Melancholy* can imagine what labor these seemingly simple changes must have required.

From the medical profession Burton's work has received very

[27] Ford, *The Plays of John Ford*, Mermaid Series, ed. by Havelock Ellis, London and New York, n.d., p. xvii.

little attention. In 1914 Sir William Osler, in an article in *The Yale Review*, insisted that the *Anatomy* was a serious psychiatric study and still of value, but, unfortunately, he never found time to demonstrate the basis for this conviction. In 1936 Dr. Joseph Miller praised Burton generously in the *Annals of Medical History*, but his account was brief and he attempted no evaluation in the light of modern psychiatry. *A History of Medical Psychology*, by Gregory Zilboorg, in collaboration with George W. Henry, published in 1941, mentions Burton, as the authority for a short quotation, in a footnote, but there is no suggestion that the authors ever conceived of his book as relevant to their subject.

The ensuing chapters seek to remedy this neglect by stating as succinctly as possible Burton's observations of the symptoms, theories of the causes, and suggestions for the treatment of a certain class of mental disturbances.

Symptomatology

THE word "melancholy," Burton confesses, is frequently used to describe the mood that accompanies "every small occasion of sorrow, need, sickness, trouble, fear, grief, passion or perturbation of the mind." But it is "improperly so called." Such a mood is an inescapable part of "the character of mortality"; whereas the condition which he proposes to discuss under the name of melancholy "is an habit, *morbus sonticus*, or *chronicus*, a chronick or continuate disease, a settled humor," not a mere pensiveness or depression of spirits, but a condition of severe mental disturbance.

He declines to attempt an exact definition, for that, he feels, would exceed the power of man: the letters of the alphabet "make no more variety of words in divers languages" than melancholy produces variety of symptoms; the tower of Babel yielded no such confusion of tongues; one could as soon understand the motion of a bird in the air as know the heart of a melancholy man; as well attempt to square the circle, rectify the Gregorian calendar or, for that matter, "make the Moon a new coat" as to give an exact description of this disease.[1] For one of its basic symptoms is a corrupt imagination, and this in itself produces a legion of others.

But he is resolved, by sheer indefatigable listing of innumerable symptoms to bring home to the reader the extent of the malady and the difficulty of dealing with it.

Give me but a little leave [he says], and I will set before your eyes in brief a stupend, vast, infinite Ocean of incredible madness and folly: a Sea full of shelves and rocks, sands, gulfs, Euripuses, and contrary tides, full of fearful monsters, uncouth shapes, roaring waves, tempests,

[1] *Anatomy*, pp. 337, 347.

and Siren calms, Halcyonian Seas, unspeakable misery, such Comedies and Tragedies, such absurd and ridiculous, feral and lamentable fits, that I know not whether they are more to be pitied or derided, or may be believed, but that we daily see the same still practised in our days, fresh examples, new news, fresh objects of misery and madness in this kind, that are still [continually] represented unto us, abroad, at home, in the midst of us, in our bosoms.[2]

He is himself almost at a loss to know how to approach a disease that manifests itself in such multifarious and contradictory ways:

In attempting to speak of these Symptoms, shall I laugh with Democritus, or weep with Heraclitus? they are so ridiculous and absurd on the one side, so lamentable and tragical on the other; a mixt Scene offers itself, so full of errors, and a promiscuous variety of objects, that I know not in what strain to represent it.[3]

Perhaps, he conjectures, the entire disease is a symptom, an indication of some deeper, mysterious sickness, of the maladjustment, it may be, of life itself to its environment.[4]

He tries to isolate it for purposes of examination from several other disturbed states that are similar in appearance. He recognizes the depressive reactions characteristic of middle and old age, for instance, but excludes them from consideration; the condition which he seeks to anatomize is a general reaction which has nothing to do with the climacterics or the changes that come with age.

The difficulty in the way of defining melancholy, he says elsewhere, is that it is "a symbolizing disease" whose true nature seeks concealment; it is protean, evading recognition in a thousand remote disguises. In other sicknesses the patient is often able to assist the diagnosis by locating his pain and describing its nature, but in this sickness "the soul is carried hoodwinkt and the understanding captive." The patient's feelings overrule his reason, and his evidence, even as to the nature of his own suffering, cannot be implicitly accepted. Furthermore, each patient's symptoms will differ, for custom, discipline, education, and individual inclinations all af-

[2] *Ibid.*, p. 868.   [3] *Ibid.*, p. 896.
[4] See pp. 91–97, where Burton's conception of the relation of culture to neurosis is presented.

fect the disease's manifestations, so that "seldom two men shall be like affected in every respect"; "scarce is there one of a thousand that dotes alike." [5]

But whether melancholy is a symptom or a disease, whether it is a cause or an effect, Burton felt that it was the most universal of afflictions: "Who is free from melancholy? Who is not touched more or less in habit or disposition?" No man living is wholly free, "no stoic, none so wise, none so happy, none so patient, so generous, so godly, so divine" that he does not at some time or other experience its transitory forms. No other misery is so widespread.

He will not recognize the dichotomy that finds popular expression today in the terms "sane" and "insane"; there are, for him, only greater or less deviations from a hypothetical norm. As melancholy he classifies the drunken, the sulky, the vain, the peevish, the extravagant, the desperate, and the harebrained. Anger and madness differ only in duration, and who can claim that he is wholly free from anger? Therefore who can claim that he is wholly free from melancholy? "In whom does not passion, envy, discontent, fear and sorrow reign?" Yet these in excess are the ingredients of mental derangement.

And who shall decide what constitutes excess? Prudence, foresight and economy, for instance, are admirable characteristics, indicative of mental health; yet they are but mild or restrained forms of pusillanimity, covetousness, and avarice—characteristics that border upon and even cross over into the realm of mental sickness.

It is in the *excess*, rather than in any particular state or condition, that Burton finds the symptom of melancholy. Hunger, for example, is natural; gluttony is a sign of melancholy. In hunger a bodily need expresses itself, and when the need is satisfied the expression disappears; but in gluttony a bodily appetite is serving as the expression of a mental need, and, since no amount of eating can ever satisfy this need, the appetite will remain insatiable.

The important point—which Burton makes with insistence—is that the common symptoms of melancholy are only exaggerations

[5] *Anatomy*, p. 327. Earlier quotations in this paragraph are from pp. 185, 347, 344, 155.

of desires or states that in moderation are universal. "Thou thyself," he says to the presumably sane reader, "art the subject of my discourse." "We have all been mad," he confesses, "at one time or another; you yourself, I think, are touched, and this man, and that man, so I must be, too." [6] Perhaps the thought comforted him; the extension of his misfortune to all men may have made him feel less alone or it may have been a form of revenge. His epitaph is proof that it afforded him some deep satisfaction.

The newly introduced cosmography of Copernicus supplied him with a droll figure with which to emphasize the universal nature of melancholy: if the earth *is* a moon, then all is explained, for its inhabitants must of necessity all be "giddy, vertiginous and lunatic within this sublunary maze." And not only as individuals are they so afflicted but also as groups and nations. Sometimes whole communities are swept into a dementia, as in the dancing manias, or as in the obsession of the Abderites with one of the choruses from the *Andromeda* of Euripides.[7] Entire kingdoms were subject to melancholy; provinces and nations could manifest the same disturbances that agitated single men and women.

But despite all this vagueness and the difficulties involved in attempting to draw any hard and fast line between the normal and the abnormal, Burton felt that it was possible to indicate some definite symptoms of melancholy. In the infinite flux there were recognizable constants and despite the thousands of idiosyncratic variations "a disagreeing likeness still."

And that disagreeing likeness was anxiety—sorrow out of proportion to any known cause, fear and sadness without apparent occasion.[8]

Sorrow is "the mother and daughter of melancholy, her epitome, symptom and chief cause." They are inseparable companions. The grief of the melancholy is of so overwhelming a character that it drowns all their other feelings. To be sure they will laugh many

[6] *Ibid.*, p. 615.
[7] *Ibid.*, pp. 124, 701. See also J. F. C. Hecker, *The Dancing Mania of the Middle Ages;* translated by B. G. Babington, New York, 1885. No. 72 in "The Humboldt Library of Science."
[8] *Anatomy*, pp. 61, 224-225, 840, 939, 946, *et passim.*

times and seem by fits and starts to be exceptionally merry, but these gay-seeming moments are only bubbles on the surface, whose direction is counter to the dark current beneath. In the midst of their despondency they may suddenly be lighthearted, but this gaiety will be transient and will stop in an instant, departing with as little evident cause as it came, leaving them lumpish and despondent again. Sorrow sticks by them continually; they cannot avoid it.

No sooner are their eyes open but, after terrible and troublesome dreams, their heavy hearts begin to sigh: they are still [continually] fretting, chafing, sighing, grieving, complaining, finding faults, repining, grudging, weeping, *Heautontimorumenoi*, vexing themselves, disquieted in mind, with restless, unquiet thoughts, discontent, either for their own, other men's, or publick affairs, such as concern them not, things past, present, or to come; the remembrance of some disgrace, loss, injury, abuse, &c. troubles them now, being idle, afresh, as if it were new done.[9]

But though this anxiety is often irrational and lacks, to the observer, sufficient justification in fact, nonetheless, it is a genuine anxiety and has a fully sufficient cause as far as the sufferer is concerned. To dismiss the woes of the neurotic as unreal because "imaginary" is, says Burton, stupid. All woes short of immediate physical pain are "imaginary." The degree of correspondence between its cause and external reality is irrelevant to the realness of the pain. And nothing can be more obtuse or less helpful than the all-too-common practice of telling the neurotic sufferer that his anxiety is groundless and therefore ridiculous. For to him it is neither groundless nor ridiculous; it is a most painful present actuality.

It is an ordinary thing [Burton observes] for such as are sound to laugh at this dejected pusillanimity, and those other symptoms of melancholy, to make themselves merry with them, and to wonder at such, as toys and trifles, which may be resisted and withstood, if they will themselves: but let him that so wonders consider with himself that, if a man should tell him on a sudden some of his especial friends were dead, could he choose but grieve? or set him upon a steep rock, where he

[9] *Ibid.*, p. 331.

should be in danger to be precipitated, could he be secure? his heart would tremble for fear, and his head be giddy. Peter Byarus gives instance (as I have said [elsewhere]): *and put case* (saith he) *in one that walks upon a plank; if it lie on the ground, he can safely do it, but if the same plank be laid over some deep water, instead of a bridge, he is vehemently moved, & 'tis nothing but his imagination,* the idea of falling being impressed upon him, *to which his other members and faculties obey.* Yea, but you infer that such men have a just cause to fear, a true object of fear; so have melancholy men an inward cause, a perpetual fume [cloud] and darkness, causing fear, grief, suspicion, which they carry with them; an object which cannot be removed, but sticks as close, and is as inseparable, as a shadow to a body, and who can expel, or over-run his shadow? [10]

Rational counsel and comfort are worse than wasted upon the melancholy. Their woes are basically irrational, and such counsel and comfort can only add to their exasperation. The whole trouble is that their imaginations are at fault. Eternal fear keeps them in eternal torment. They are "restless and distracted." They cannot eat or drink or sleep in the continual apprehension of their own self-tormentings.

They are headstrong and passionate. "What they desire, they do most furiously seek." They are envious, malicious, and suspicious, alternating between fits of impulsive generosity and mistrustful niggardliness. They are covetous and greedy; indeed, the immoderate desire of gain may be regarded as "the pattern, image, epitome of all Melancholy." [11]

They are likely to be surly in common social relationships and sullen in conversation, yet they are not stupid, but capable of deep and cunning thoughts. They are often judicious and wise, but they spoil the effect of their wisdom by obstinacy and capricious perversity. They are inclined to be witty, sometimes extremely so; but at the same time they deeply resent a jest at their expense. They are oversensitive, "cholerick, apt to mistake," supposing offenses where none are intended. They aggravate a joke and brood over it until it becomes a perpetual corrosive to them; there can be "no

[10] *Ibid.,* pp. 358–359. [11] *Ibid.,* pp. 245, 334.

jesting with a discontented person." "If they have been misused, derided, disgraced, chidden, etc., or by any perturbation of mind misaffected, it so far troubles them, that they become quite moped many times, and so disheartened, dejected, they dare not come abroad."

They exaggerate all fears and misfortunes, particularly the symptoms of any sickness they may have; it is "a common fault of all melancholy persons" so to do. "They complain, weep, lament, and think they lead a most miserable life; never was any man so bad, or so before, every poor man they see is most fortunate in respect to them, every beggar that comes to the door is happier than they are." [12]

They torment themselves with absurd and brainsick questions. If any small circumstance in their affairs is omitted or forgotten, "they are miserably tormented, and frame [conceive] a thousand dangers and inconveniences to themselves." Some slip of the tongue or accidental breach of manners that would merely annoy or embarrass another person dejects them beyond all measure. They cannot forget it and suffer agonies of shame long after the incident has been forgotten by everyone else.

Here, again, the symptom lies in the excess. The impulses and fears that pass fleetingly through every mind seem to find permanent lodgment in theirs and grow there to irresistible force and insurmountable size.

Some of the reactions which Burton describes would today be regarded as characteristic of other types of psychological disturbance than melancholia. From his authors he collects many illustrations of hallucinations, perversions, and compulsions. One man hears frogs in his belly. Another is convinced that he is made of butter and shuns all warmth for fear of melting. One woman must wash her hair every day. Some patients believe that they have swallowed something loathsome. Many are convinced that their relatives are trying to kill them. Some dare not leave their houses "through bashfulness, suspicion and timorousness." Still others dare not open their mouths "lest in some inappropriate place they sud-

[12] *Ibid.*, p. 332.

denly speak out some indecency." "One supposeth himself to be a lord, a Duke, a Prince. And if he be told he hath a stinking breath, a great nose, that he is sick, or inclined to such or such a disease, he believes it eftsoons, and peradventure, by force of imagination, will work it out."

But although Burton classifies these acts and states as indicative of melancholy, he includes them largely for their value as diversion or amusement and does not attempt to fit them into his basic theories. They were all things that he had read, not observed or experienced.

Of more importance, more central to his interest, was the melancholy man's loss of object relationship, his marked inability to do "that which concerns him." Burton had observed that the melancholy, though they undertake a score of projects, often with vigor, accomplish little. They seem to be restrained from accomplishing their desires by some supposed impossibility. Though they may have talents of a high order, they can make little use of them, for the perpetual fear which makes them timorous prevents them from entering successfully into the human relationships which are involved in almost any performance. They are thwarted by their own restlessness and impatience. They find it very difficult to get on with people; they will abuse their best friends or even offer them violence, upon small or no provocation, and at the same time they are afraid to do anything that might offend their enemies.

Suspicion and *jealousy* are general symptoms: they are commonly distrustful, timorous, apt to mistake, and amplify, testy, pettish, peevish, and ready to snarl upon every small occasion, with their greatest friends, and without a cause, given or not given, it will be to their offense. If they speak in jest, he takes it in good earnest. If they be not saluted, invited, consulted with, called to counsel, &c. or that any respect, small compliment, or ceremony be omitted, they think themselves neglected and contemned [despised]: for a time that tortures them. If two talk together, discourse, whisper, jest, or tell a tale in general, he thinks presently [immediately] they mean him, applies all to himself. Or if they talk with him, he is ready to misconstrue every word they speak, and interpret it to the worst; he cannot endure any man to look steadily on him, speak to him almost, laugh, jest, or be familiar, or hem, or point, cough, or spit, or make a noise sometimes, &c. He thinks they laugh or point at him, or do it in disgrace of him, circumvent him, contemn him; every man looks at him, he is pale, red, sweats for fear and anger, lest some body should observe him. He works upon it, and long after this false conceit [imagination] of an abuse troubles him. . . .

Inconstant they are in all their actions, vertiginous, restless, unapt to resolve of any business, they will and will not, persuaded to and fro upon every small occasion, or word spoken; and yet, if once they be resolved, obstinate, hard to be reconciled; if they abhor, dislike, or distaste, once settled, though to the better, by no odds, counsel or persuasion to be removed; yet in most things wavering, irresolute, unable to deliberate, through fear. Now prodigal, and then covetous, they do, and by-and-by repent them of that which they have done, so that both ways they are troubled, whether they do or do not, want or have, hit or miss, disquieted of all hands, soon weary, and still seeking change, restless, I say, fickle, fugitive, they may not abide to tarry in one place long . . . no company long, or to persevere in any action or business.[13]

For such unhappy beings there is, naturally, little hope of pleasure in either work or play.

As a man that's bitten with fleas, or that cannot sleep, turns to and fro in his bed, their restless minds are tossed & vary, they have no patience to read out a book, to play out a game or two, walk a mile, sit an hour, &c. erected and dejected in an instant: animated to undertake, and upon a word spoken again[st] discouraged.[14]

Suspicion poisons their every association. The melancholy man "hunts after every whisper and amplifies it to himself with a most unjust calumny of others." "He pries into every corner, follows close, observes to an hair," eternally seeking something to justify his resentments.

The melancholy are always aggressive: "they cannot speak but they must bite." [15] But they do not perceive that they are aggressive, feeling, rather, that they are always being attacked, "as they that drink wine think all runs round, when it is in their own brain."

[13] *Ibid.*, pp. 332–333.   [14] *Ibid.*   [15] *Ibid.*, p. 290.

They are bored, weary of life. "Their days pass wearily by, they are soon tired with all things." They show "rather a necessity to live than a desire." They are restless, "disquieted, perplexed"; "they will now tarry, now be gone, now up, then go to bed; now pleased, then again displeased; now they like, by and by dislike all, weary of all."

They are capricious beyond measure, at one moment laughing profusely and at the next weeping bitterly. Their moods change abruptly and tend to extremes: "A poor fellow went to hang himself . . . but, finding by chance a pot of money, flung away the rope, and went merrily home; but he that hid the gold, when he missed it, hanged himself with that rope which the other man had left." [16]

Since melancholy is a disease of soul *and* body, in which heart and brain "mutually misaffect one another," there are physical as well as mental and emotional symptoms. For as "the distraction and distemper of the body will cause a distemperature of the soul," so "the distraction of the mind, amongst other outward causes & perturbations, alters the temperature [the general health] of the body." Each receives a tincture from the other, "as wine savours of the cask wherein it is kept," and " 'tis hard to decide which of these two will do more harm to the other." [17]

But the physical symptoms were to Burton of secondary significance—a point on which he differed from most of his learned authors, to most of whom the physical disfunctions were causes of the mental disturbances with which they were concomitant. Burton granted that a disturbance of certain physical functions usually attended mental disturbances, that a prolonged disturbance of these functions might lead to distinct organic changes which would constitute sickness in themselves, and that the sickness so caused was a genuine physical sickness and must be treated as such. But the psychological disturbance, he insisted, was antecedent,[18] and no permanent cure of the secondary sickness could be effected until the primary disturbance was cured. This belief was basic in his etiology and in his therapy.

[16] *Ibid.*, p. 308.   [17] *Ibid.*, pp. 318, 319.   [18] *Ibid.*, pp. 217–224.

With this reservation he is quite willing, however, to list certain physical conditions as symptoms of melancholy. The patients are pale and sallow. They suffer from insomnia. Some of them stutter. Most of them are continually tired, easily exhausted, plagued with flatulence and other digestive disorders. "Melancholy men," he had observed, "most part have good appetites, but ill digestion." [19]

And in addition to the symptoms of physical disturbances which they actually have, they may manifest the symptoms of other ailments which their fears have led them to think they have, for their imaginations are in nothing more active than in conceiving illnesses and misfortunes, and once they believe that they have a certain disease, they will, says Burton, by force of imagination produce its symptoms.

Whether by this he meant that they would actually have the symptoms or only the simulation of them is not quite clear. One or two passages in the *Anatomy* suggest that he believed that a psychological disturbance could produce a definite physical change. He states, for instance, that the stigmata of St. Francis of Assisi were the products of melancholy. But it is difficult to ascertain from the passage whether he thought St. Francis' melancholy had produced a somatic change or whether he thought that the melancholy of St. Francis' disciples had led them to imagine that they saw the stigmata. [20]

But, as has been said, he is less concerned with the physical symptoms than with the emotional, of which fear and sorrow are the chief. That of the many manifestations of fear and sorrow, feelings of guilt seemed to weigh so heavily on the melancholy was a fact which struck him most forcefully. They endure the "most intolerable torment and insufferable anguish of conscience." Excessive moral scruples threaten and frustrate them at every turn. They reproach themselves ceaselessly "and aggravate every small offense, when there is no such cause." The enormity of their wickedness, "the intolerable burden of their sins," oppresses them night and day. [21]

[19] *Ibid.*, p. 400. Earlier references in this paragraph are to pp. 326, 327, 605.
[20] *Ibid.*, pp. 335, 895.   [21] *Ibid.*, pp. 939, 945, 951, *et passim.*

They are superstitious, attaching tremendous importance to details of ceremonial and seeing in every event an omen or a warning. The slightest deviation from a prescribed ritual plunges them into dejection and self-reproach. They cannot endure the least omission from an established form.

> They dare not break the least ceremony, tradition, edict: hold it a greater sin to eat a bit of meat in Lent than kill a man: their consciences are so terrified, that they are ready to despair if a small ceremony be omitted; and will accuse their own Father, Mother, Brother, Sister, nearest and dearest friends, of heresy, if they do not as they do, will be their chief executioners, and help first to bring a fagot to burn them.[22]

They delight in expiations and will voluntarily undergo penances which no "power of Prince, or penal law" could ever force them to endure.

And, naturally, so burdened with a sense of sin, they seek the consolations of religion—or, rather, the horrors of religion, for its consolations are not for them; in their dejection, feeling that they are rejected, they assume that there is no more hope for them in the next world than in this.

In the sixteenth and seventeenth centuries neurotic guilt must have invariably taken the form of religious guilt, and the churches furnished those so afflicted with a most dreadful series of punitive torments on which to meditate. The gloomy fatalism of Calvinism, in particular, offered confirmation to the blackest despair. The agonies of hell and the implacable nature of God's "justice" were the commonest of all themes in the sermons of the day, and at that time sermons carried an authority of which an enlightened person today can scarcely conceive. The suffering that these doctrines, and especially the lurid and detailed descriptions of the torments of the damned that always embellished them, must have caused among the depressed and the emotionally unstable staggers the imagination. The journals of eyewitnesses are endless catalogues of contortions, convulsions, cataleptic seizures, faintings, and hys-

[22] *Ibid.*, p. 915.

terical screamings of the "doomed" at the picture of their future which the eloquent divines so vividly portrayed.[23]

To Burton's credit as a minister it must be said that he regarded all such proceedings with the sternest disapproval. If his knowledge of divinity helped him in his particular medical studies, his knowledge of medicine helped him no less in his ministerial capacity. "Nothing," he maintains stoutly, "more besots and infatuates men, does more harm, works more disquietude to mankind" than playing on morbid fears in the name of religion. It has "more crucified the souls of men than wars, plagues, sickness, death, famine, and all the rest." Perhaps here, as in so many passages in the *Anatomy*, he is speaking from his own painful experience.

At first, as he knew, melancholy could be most pleasant. To lie in bed whole days and keep one's chamber, "to walk alone in some solitary grove, betwixt wood and water, by a brookside, to meditate upon some delightsome and pleasant subject" could be "a most incomparable delight." "To melancholize and build castles in the air!" To spend whole days and nights in "contemplations and fantastical meditations!" Nor were the pleasures purely imaginary; the state of being melancholy was in itself at first a pleasure: "The imagination, inwardly or outwardly moved, represents to the understanding, not enticements only, to favor the passion, or dislike, but a very intensive pleasure follows the passion, or displeasure, and the will and reason are captivated by delighting in it." [24]

But the end of these pleasures is pain—pain more excruciating than can be conceived by those who have not felt it, the most insufferable anguish known to men. Some have questioned whether the diseases of the body or the diseases of the mind are more grievous. Burton laughs at the ignorance that could raise the question: "there is no comparison, no doubt to be made of it, the diseases of the mind are far more grievous." The melancholy man is "the cream of human adversity, the quintessence, the upshot; all other diseases whatever are but fleabitings."

[23] See chap. iv of Gilbert Seldes, *The Stammering Century*, New York, 1928; and see chap. iv and Appendix V of J. F. C. Hecker, *The Dancing Mania of the Middle Ages*, for even more recent eyewitness accounts.
[24] *Anatomy*, pp. 214, 359–360.

. . . imagine what thou canst, fear, sorrow, furies, grief, pain, terror, anger, dismal, ghastly, tedious, irksome, &c., it is not sufficient, it comes far short, no tongue can tell, no heart conceive it. 'Tis an Epitome of hell, an extract, a quintessence, a compound, a mixture of all feral maladies, tyrannical tortures, plagues and perplexities. There is no sickness, almost, but Physick provideth a remedy for it; to every sore Chirurgery will provide a salve: friendship helps poverty; hope of liberty easeth imprisonment; suit and favour revoke banishment; authority and time wear away reproach: but what Physick, what Chirurgery, what wealth, favour, authority can relieve, bear out, assuage, or expel a troubled conscience? A quiet mind cureth all them, but all they cannot comfort a distressed soul: who can put to silence the voice of desperation? . . . They are in great pain and horror of mind, distraction of soul, restless, full of continual fears, cares, torments, anxieties, they can neither eat, drink, nor sleep for them, take no rest . . . Fear takes away their content, and dries the blood, wasteth the marrow, alters their countenance, even in their greatest delights, singing, dancing, dalliance, they are still (saith Lemnius) tortured in their souls.[25]

Whatever doubts there may have been about the proper treatment for those in this wretched state, Burton maintained that there could be no question of one thing: their feelings of guilt and their dread of punishment ought not to be *increased*. In fact, if something were not done to mitigate these feelings, if the sense of guilt were not in some manner alleviated, the victims were likely to sink into complete despair, isolated beyond the reach of all comfort or advice, alone in the blackness of their self-reproach and fear, the most utterly miserable of created things.

No wonder that those who reach this dreadful state so often seek to destroy themselves and "offer violence to their own persons," for black choler "is a shoeing horn to suicide." The afflicted wretches feel that only death can bring them ease, and in the very act of destroying themselves they will have some sort of revenge against circumstances.

They are afraid of death, and yet weary of their lives; in their discontented humours they quarrel with all the world, bitterly inveigh,

[25] *Ibid.*, pp. 946–947.

tax satirically, and because they cannot otherwise vent their passions, or redress what is amiss, as they mean [desire], they will by violent death at last be revenged on themselves.[26]

Not all self-destruction, however, takes the form of suicide; some stops short at self-mutilation or finds a surrogate grave in monastic retirement, complete seclusion, or absorption in some eternal ritual. But, whatever form it takes, it is, like the other manifestations of melancholy, only an exaggeration or an intensification of a "normal" tendency. For every man, says Burton, is "the greatest enemy unto himself. We study many times to undo ourselves, abusing those good things which God hath bestowed upon us, health, wealth, strength, wit, learning, art, memory, to our own destruction; you owe to yourself your own ruin." [27]

Burton classifies despair as the ultimate stage of religious melancholy, and religious melancholy he classifies as a form of love melancholy. The logic of this classification is a curious and illuminating example of the manner in which different ages express a truth in the terminology of different concepts. For the despair felt by those who have advanced to the terrible extreme of religious melancholy was, basically, he felt, due to a sense of the deprivation of love—of God's love—and their emotions were similar, though infinitely worse in degree, to those experienced by anyone who had been rejected by some earthly lover. Now, nothing is more common in the language of the New Testament and in the forms of the Christian church, of which he was a minister, than the thought of God as a Father, the all-loving Parent. So much is made of this, in fact, that it is inconceivable that it did not, at least unconsciously, affect his thinking, so that, in the last analysis, he traces despair not only to a denial of love but also to the denial of the love of the parent to the child.

That the section on love melancholy, of which the section on religious melancholy is a subdivision, occupies almost a third of the entire *Anatomy of Melancholy* is, again, most interesting; it is significant that he felt disturbances in matters of sex to be so important to his subject and perceived that in the melancholy these

---

[26] *Ibid.*, p. 353.   [27] *Ibid.*, p. 118.

disturbances were not confined to the sexual union, but were ex-
tended to the whole process of objectizing love. Disturbances in
sexual love he saw as but one manifestation of some profound
thwarting or damming up of the whole current of life in the suf-
ferers; other manifestations which he noted were their inability to
exercise their talents fruitfully, their continual self-frustrations,
their conflicts with others, particularly with those emotionally
close to them, and the various ways and degrees in which they
sought to destroy themselves.

The melancholy, then, which Burton sought to analyze is a condition which he discriminates from ordinary lowness of spirits by
its fixed or chronic nature and by the fact that it does not proceed,
or does not seem to proceed, from normal or "rational" causes. He
does not set it apart from certain other psychopathic states as
clearly as modern psychiatry does, but he distinguishes it ex-
plicitly from febrile delirium and from senile dementia.

He does not attempt to define it closely, because by its very
nature it defies close definition. It is a symbolizing disease, expressing itself according to the personality and environment of the patient in diverse symptoms, of which fear and sorrow "out of proportion with the known causes" are the chief. Those afflicted are
restless, emotionally unstable, inclined to be greedy and covetous,
ill-tempered and aggressive. They are particularly disturbed in
their sexual relations, using the term in its widest possible sense.
They are eternally tormented with feelings of guilt, oppressed
with a sense of their own unworthiness and the belief that they
are rejected and despised. These feelings, unless assuaged, progress
to despair, from which they seek deliverance—and at the same
time a sort of revenge—through self-destruction.

Etiology

THE introspection which furnished Burton with so much knowledge of the symptoms of melancholy was not of any great value
in enlightening him as to its causes, though it was not utterly
worthless, and his honesty and intelligence enabled him to make
the most of what it could suggest.

Most of the authors whom he had read attributed melancholy
to some physical cause. Burton felt that they were wrong; he
granted that mental and physical illnesses were often interrelated,
but, as has been said, he did not believe that any physical condition
could be regarded as the primary cause of melancholy. Nonetheless
he felt it incumbent upon him, as a definite part of "anatomizing,"
to arrange and present the vast mass of medical opinion supporting
physical causes. His discursive habit of mind, however, made him
a poor arranger, and, even if he had been efficient and precise, his
efforts in this particular division of his work would not have been,
by our standards, of much use. For at the time at which he began
his work, medical thinking was still dominated by the classical
concepts of the four humors and the natural, vital, and animal
spirits.

Modern medicine, it is true, was already beginning: Vesalius,
Pare, and Weyer had done their work before he was out of his
childhood; Harvey and Sydenham were his contemporaries; and
the ideas which were to inspire Boerhaave and Hales in the next
generation were current before he died. But these men were innovators, and although Burton himself was an innovator in some
things, in physiology and anatomy he adhered to the established
orthodoxy. He was quite willing to believe that the liver heated

the stomach "as a fire doth a kettle," that the function of the venosa artery was to fetch air from the lungs "to refrigerate the heart," and that laughter was caused by "an abundance of pleasant vapours which, proceeding from the heart, tickle the midriff." For were not these things in every book, vouched for by every authority from Aristotle down?

In astrology, which was then as closely related to medicine as chemistry now is, he was plainly more than a follower of the times. Wood says that he was "an exact calculator of nativities," and we know what importance the Oxford gossips thought that he attached to his own horoscope. Yet his faith is not absolute. In the *Anatomy* he hedges a little; he will not definitely commit himself. The stars "incline" those with a predisposition to melancholy, he says, but they do not compel them, and they incline so gently that it is within our power to resist them; the stars rule us, but "God rules them," and we are answerable only to God.

If this seems equivocal or confusing, we must by an act of imagination transfer ourselves to the pre-Newtonian world, a world which had not yet been arranged upon the deceptively simple plan of "natural laws," a world whose awe and mystery had not yet been removed to the safe distance of the nebulae, but crept about in everyday life like a fog, obscuring the obvious, distorting the familiar, and enlarging men and women into terrible forms and shapes. The unknown was very near, and fear moved uneasily just beneath the surface of familiar things.

And if the age seems preposterously gullible about accepting whatever it found in print, we must by the same act of imagination transfer ourselves from our world of books, newspapers, magazines, advertisements, libraries, interoffice communications, and so forth, to a world in which nine men out of ten could not read at all. Reading and writing were once next door to the black arts; the mystery that surrounded them survives in the meanings of "runes," "glamor," and "authority." By Burton's time all sense of magic had long since faded from writing, but, even so, the printed page was regarded with a veneration that owed some of its force to the older feeling. The sanctity of the Bible may well have had something to do with it, but at any rate those who spoke through books were not to be lightly challenged; their very saying so was, in a measure, evidence for what they said. Thus, when the great Sckenkius affirmed that he had seen "little things like whelps" in the urine of those stricken with hydrophobia, his very affirmation constituted, to Burton, a medical fact and as such had to be recorded, as indeed—though perhaps for different reasons—it should have been.

To ask of any man other than the most exceptional—the Leonardo, the Bacon, the Freud—that he divest himself of the concepts of his age is to ask the impossible. A man of the sixteenth and seventeenth centuries could no more have disregarded the authority of books than a man of the twentieth century could cease to believe in the relation of cause and effect or in the actuality of his own sense impressions.

And so it was also with the belief that certain mental disturbances had a supernatural origin. It may be confidently asserted that at the beginning of the seventeenth century no one of any intellectual prominence whatever doubted that at least some forms of insanity were caused by devils. For one thing, such a doubt would have required a flat contradiction of the factual accuracy of the Bible.[1] Pope Innocent VIII, in his bull *Summis desiderantes affectibus*, had declared a disbelief in diabolical possession to be "unblushing effrontery,"[2] and, in this, at least, there can be no doubt that he had the hearty concurrence of Luther and Calvin.

Of course, there was considerable difference of opinion as to *how* the devils operated. Some thought that they lived inside the afflicted persons and by their actual physical presence and move-

[1] See Gen. 6:4; Exod. 22:18; Levit. 19:31; 20:6, 27; Deut. 18:10; I Sam. 18:10; 28:3–20; Matt. 4:24; 8:16, 28–33; Mark 16:9; Luke 4:41; 8:2, 27–36; Acts 16:16–18; Gal. 5:20; *et passim.* Blackstone, *Commentaries,* 1765, IV, 60, says, "To deny the possibility, nay, the actual existence of witchcraft and sorcery is . . . flatly to contradict the revealed Word of God." John Wesley firmly maintained that certain hysterical phenomena were due to the presence of devils inside the afflicted person, and to the end of his life insisted that "the giving up of witchcraft is in effect giving up the Bible." Lecky, *Rationalism in Europe,* rev. ed., New York, I, 139, 140, 151.
[2] Zilboorg, *A History of Medical Psychology,* p. 150.

ments caused the nausea, borborygmus, tympany, convulsions—
or whatever the symptom might be. Others thought that the devils
worked from the outside, frightening the patient into manifest-
ing these symptoms by sudden appearances or whispered suggestions. Still others—probably the majority—thought that the devils
did their work through the mediation of witches, who had the
power to bind and influence people by means of spells. And each
group, needless to say, found full confirmation for its particular
theory in Holy Writ, in secular authorities, and in the voluminous
testimony of the afflicted.

There were protests, but they were directed more against this
or that theory of causation than against the basic idea. Even the
most enlightened and humane thinkers of the day, the German
Johan Weyer and the Englishman Reginald Scot,[3] did not go so
far as to doubt *all* demoniacal possession. Their efforts were directed chiefly against the mounting hysteria and sadism of the
witch hunters; they did not seek so much to deny the possibility
of a man's being inhabited by a devil as to insist that, if he were,
it was a misfortune, not a crime.

But even this limited skepticism aroused the anger of all "right-
minded" men. King James the First (whom the Devil frankly acknowledged to be "the greatest enemy he hath in the worlde" [4])
condemned the tenets of both Scot and Weyer as "damnable opinions," and one of his first acts upon ascending the English throne
was to enact a law condemning witches to death upon the first

[3] For Weyer, see A. D. White, *History of the Warfare of Science with
Theology in Christendom*, New York, 1926, I, 359; Lecky, *History . . .
of Rationalism in Europe*, New York, 1870, I, 105-107; Montague Summers's
Preface to his ed. of Reginald Scot, *The Discoverie of Witchcraft*, n.p., 1930,
and, particularly, Gregory Zilboorg, *The Medical Man and the Witch during
the Renaissance*, New York, 1935, chap. v. See also Zilboorg, *A History of
Medical Psychology*, pp. 207-235. The history of the struggle for intellectual
freedom is indebted to Zilboorg for calling attention to Weyer's true great-
ness, but his enthusiasm leads him to claim for the author of the *De praestigiis
daemonum* a point of view which would have been impossible in sixteenth-
century Europe. See what Burton says, *Anatomy*, pp. 175-176. For Scot,
see Montague Summers's edition of the *Discoverie*, particularly the Preface;
and see Lecky, *History . . . of Rationalism in Europe*, I, 122-123.

[4] See a curious little pamphlet *Newes from Scotland*, 1591, Bodley Head reprint, Oxford, 1924. And see James's own *Daemonologie*, 1597, Bodley Head
reprint, Oxford, 1924.

conviction. This law, as Lecky has pointed out,[5] was passed when Coke was attorney general and Bacon a member of parliament. Twelve bishops sat upon the commission to which it was referred. Nor can it be claimed that men of this caliber probably held other views and were being discreetly silent. In *The Advancement of Learning* Bacon lists witchcraft as one of the three "declinations from religion." The learned Hales, the judicial Selden, the grave Glanvil, More, and Cudworth, the Cambridge Platonists—all men of the highest intellectual powers—believed in witchcraft and believed that it was responsible for most of the phenomena that are now classified as neurotic or psychotic symptoms. To have questioned so evident, so "established" a fact would indeed have marked a man, in the phrase of the pious Baxter, as "a very obdurate Sadducee."

The very mention of Weyer and Scot serves, in a way, to distort the actual picture of the scene in which Burton lived. Because their opinions agree, in part, with ours, and because they were pioneers in what we regard as the truth, we are inclined to magnify them and to assume that their ideas must have provoked a major controversy. Whereas actually they were less significant then than now; the common man, we may be sure, never heard of them, and to most of the learned their opinions must have seemed only the ravings of lunatics or the blasphemies of infidels.

Nothing more illuminates the common attitude toward devils than the nonchalance with which their appearance is alluded to, even by some of the most respected men of the day. Jerome Cardan, for example, solemnly asserts that on the thirteenth of August, 1491, his father, "after the accustomed solemnities," conjured up "seven devils in Greek apparel." He distinctly remembers that the spirits seemed about forty years of age, "some ruddy and some pale." Devils were not an unfamiliar sight in the Cardan household; his father, he adds casually, had one "bound to him as an apprentice for twenty and eight years." [6]

[5] Lecky, *op. cit.*, I, 123, 140, 151. The last legal execution for witchcraft in England took place in 1712, though on the continent these judicial murders continued for seventy years after that. Our grandfathers could have known men who had seen men and women hanged for associating with the devil.

[6] *Anatomy*, pp. 161, 167.

And Cardan was not alone. Burton quotes the testimony of Paracelsus to show that devils were abundant in Germany, where "they do usually walk in little coats some two foot long." In this he is borne out by "that holy man Ketellus," who had "an especial grace to see devils and talk with them." Ketellus, who had become almost avuncular in his attitude toward sprites, says that these little ones are more mischievous than harmful; they love, he says, to sit by the highway and frighten horses in order to laugh at the discomfiture of the riders.[7]

Such a spirit it was, perhaps, that appeared to John Jorden and John Sheerman in 1599, "about a foot high, white on the top, which had an audible voice." [8] And they kept on appearing all through Burton's lifetime and long after. "*Anno* 1670," John Aubrey records in his *Miscellanies*, "not far from Cirencester, was an apparition: being demanded, whether a good spirit, or a bad? returned no answer, but disappeared with a curious perfume and most melodious twang." [9] Aubrey does not seem to doubt the actuality of the fragrant specter; his concern is almost wholly with its proper classification.

Now religion, folklore, and a great deal of the best medical thinking of the time connected demons particularly with those personality problems which we today regard as neurotic in character: hysteria, anxiety, and (as anyone knows who is familiar with the literature of witchcraft or, let us say, the engravings of Jacques Callot or those of Hieronymus Bosch) with sadism and other sexual abnormalities.

Impulses toward suicide were thought especially to be the work of the devil, since self-destruction meant the loss of the soul as well as the body. He was believed to be constantly at the side of the depressed, urging the final counsel of despair and even facilitating its execution. Thus Edgar, in *King Lear*, disguised as Poor Tom, the bedlam beggar, sobs out that the foul fiend had laid knives under his pillow, hung halters in his pew, and set ratsbane

[7] *Ibid.*, pp. 168, 171.
[8] Ewen, *Witchcraft and Demonianism*, London, 1933, p. 188.
[9] John Aubrey, *Miscellanies*, London, 1696; 5th ed., London, 1890, p. 81.

by his porridge in a ceaseless attempt to persuade him to kill himself. And when in the same play the mutilated Gloster tries to throw himself over a cliff, he is brought to a more pious frame of mind by being told that the idea had been suggested to him by a fiend, which his blindness had prevented him from seeing.[10]

Thus, as representatives of forbidden urges, as punitive agents, and as incentors to self-destruction, devils were too firmly established in the psychological theories of the age to be disregarded by anyone who sought to understand the causes of neuroses. Burton has been repeatedly accused of credulity for discussing them at all, but the noteworthy thing is not that he discusses them, but that in conclusion he contents himself with the evasive assertion that the whole thing "is a serious question and worthy to be considered."

Actually, however, for all the space he gives them, devils play a very small part in his etiology, because ultimately he classifies them as contributing factors. Like the stars, they incline rather than compel, and even then they can incline only those who have a favorable predisposition.

In his rather cumbrous scheme they are "non-natural"—that is, not innate—causes. With them he classifies various physical illnesses and misfortunes, such as jaundice, amenorrhea, constipation, the menopause, injuries to the head, and deficiencies or excesses of diet. Many of his authors felt that these things must be the direct causes of the mental disturbances with which they were so often connected, but Burton felt that they served only to stimulate those "perturbations and passions" which, when uncontrolled, distort the imagination and so set in motion a train of causes whose effects are the symptoms of melancholy.

Of these perturbations and passions he says:

Perturbations and passions, which trouble the phantasy, though they dwell between the confines of sense [feeling] and reason, yet they rather follow [are influenced by] sense than reason, because they are drowned in corporeal organs of sense. They are commonly reduced

[10] Shakespeare, *King Lear*, Act III, Scene 4, ll. 51–60; Act IV, Scene 6, ll. 69–79.

into two inclinations, *irascible,* and *concupiscible* . . . and if they be immoderate, they consume the spirits, and melancholy is especially caused by them. Some few discreet men there are, that can govern themselves, and curb in these inordinate affections, by religion, philosophy, and such divine precepts, of meekness, patience, and the like; but most part, for want of government [self-control], out of indiscretion, ignorance, they suffer themselves wholly to be led by sense, and are so far from repressing rebellious inclinations, that they give all encouragement unto them, leaving the reins, and using all provocations to further them: bad by nature, worse by art, discipline [teaching], custom, education, and a perverse will of their own, they follow on, wheresoever their unbridled affections will transport them, and do more out of custom, self-will, than out of reason. This stubborn will of ours, as Melancthon calls it, perverts judgment, which sees and knows what should and ought to be done, and yet will not do it. Slaves to their several [individual] lusts and appetite, they precipitate and plunge themselves into a labyrinth of cares, blinded with lust, blinded with ambition; *they seek that at God's hands which they may give unto themselves, if they could but refrain from those cares and perturbations, wherewith they continually macerate their minds.* But giving way to these violent passions of fear, grief, shame, revenge, hatred, malice, &c., they are torn in pieces, as Actæon was with his dogs, and crucify their own souls.[11]

Though the latter end of this passage tends to be slightly condemnatory, as if Burton blamed neurotics for not choosing to be more stable, yet his general meaning is clear and striking. The important cause of melancholy, he plainly states, is *inward.* Devils, sickness, and misfortunes are but contributory factors. The "phantasy" or imagination is troubled by emotions that are completely submerged ("drowned") in the sensual organs, beyond the reach of reason, particularly when these emotions are uncontrolled.

Thus the melancholy carry the source of their own misery with them. Outward causes serve only as irritants.

But, since not all men are precipitated into melancholy by their emotional excesses, some other factor must be at work in certain

[11] *Anatomy,* pp. 224–225. The italics are not for emphasis, but to mark a passage which Burton has translated from the Latin.

cases. Burton admits this. Some, he says, have a predisposition. Underlying the perturbations and passions he sees three deeper causes: heredity, lack of affection in childhood, and sexual frustration. They are not necessarily distinct and separate, but may be mingled in varying proportions, each exacerbating the other.

The first is the most important. Such as are born of melancholy parents are most likely to be melancholy. We inherit our infirmities, says Burton, as we inherit our lands—though we may have our own particular symptoms.

Of the second underlying cause, the lack of affection in childhood, he speaks, as has been said, with such feeling that there can be no doubt that he speaks from experience. Children live "in perpetual slavery" to their masters and their parents. They take for granted affronts and indignities which an adult would regard as intolerable. With one of those brilliant flashes of insight that demonstrate the sound intelligence that underlay his affectations and pedantry, he perceived that neurosis begets neurosis: "Our own parents," he cries in a moving passage, "by their offences, indiscretion, and intemperance, are our mortal enemies . . . they torment us, & we are ready to injure our posterity." [12]

Emotionally unstable parents and cruel tutors and schoolmasters are the "fountains and furtherers of melancholy." They "offend many times in that they are too stern, always threatening, chiding, brawling, whipping, or striking; by means of which their poor children are so disheartened and cowed, that they never after have any courage, a merry hour in their lives, or take pleasure in anything." [13]

Other parents and guardians "do as great harm by their too much remissness." They give their children no bringing up, teach them no trade, do not encourage them to assume responsibility. They feed their whims and smile indulgently upon their misdemeanors. Fond mothers, especially, "dote so much upon their children, like Aesop's Ape, till in the end they crush them to death." Such children, as they grow up, are inclined to become wanton, stubborn, wilful, and disobedient.[14] "There is a great moderation to be had

[12] *Ibid.*, p. 117. [13] *Ibid.*, p. 284. [14] *Ibid.*, p. 285.

in such things, as matters of so great a moment in the making or marring of a child."

Disastrous in this connection is the foolish custom, particularly common among ignorant nurses, of frightening children with terrible tales, either for amusement or to make them behave. Such practices, says Burton, are most reprehensible. Children's fears exceed the comprehension of stupid and unimaginative adults; they are "most pernicious and violent, and so suddenly alter the whole temperature of the body, move the soul & spirits, and strike such a deep impression" that the victims "can never be recovered, causing more grievous and fiercer Melancholy." [15]

What children really need is love. And not only children but adults as well. To be unloved or unloving was to be melancholy. Ultimately he regarded love—at least adult love for adults—as sexual desire. He knew, or professed to know, the romantic delights of love, but he entertained no romantic conception of their origin. Love was a physical urge, a natural appetite. "Youth is a very combustible matter"—and that's all there was to it. They are aptest to love, not that have the finest souls, but "that are young and lusty, live at ease, stall-fed, free from cares." In those of the right age who are free from any restraining conflict, love is a bodily function: "It is impossible for two young folks, equal in years, to live together, and not be in love." [16]

The charms and beauties, the virtues and graces, which the enraptured lover always insists on as the justification of his passion are commonly rationalizations. The body desires, and the mind finds reasons, sweeping away all restraints and ignoring all imperfections. Normal aesthetic standards seem not only distorted by those in love but also, often, utterly inverted:

If she be flat-nosed, she is lovely; if hook-nosed, kingly; if dwarfish and little, pretty; if tall, proper and man-like, our brave British Boadicea; if crooked, wise; if monstrous, comely; her defects are no defects at all, she hath no deformities. Though she be nasty, fulsome, as Sostratus's bitch, or Parmeno's sow: thou hadst as lieve have a snake in thy bosom, a toad in thy dish, and callest her witch, devil, hag, with all the filthy

[15] *Ibid.*, p. 286.   [16] *Ibid.*, pp. 618, 661.

names thou canst invent; he admires her, on the other side, she is his Idol, Lady, Mistress, Venerilla [or Little Venus], Queen, the quintessence of beauty, an Angel, a Star, a Goddess. . . . The fragrancy of a thousand Courtesans is in her face: 'tis not Venus' picture that, nor the Spanish Infanta's as you suppose (good Sir) no Princess, or King's daughter; no, no, but his divine Mistress forsooth, his dainty Dulcinea, his dear Antiphila, to whose service he is wholly consecrate, whom he alone adores.[17]

That the emotion of love was basically physical did not, however, lessen or restrict its scope. On the contrary, it broadened it. Love, as Burton saw it, was the common denominator of life, operating in animals and vegetables as well as in human beings. Love was not sexual desire alone, but all desire. He saw ambition, covetousness, self-love, vanity, *and* the love of a man for a woman all as manifestations of one basic urge. "Love is the circle equant of all other affections." Love is gregariousness and binds societies together. Love "built cities, invented arts, sciences, and all good things." It is "the beginner and end of all our actions." It incites us "to virtue and humanity." It underlies all pleasures and makes the pains of life endurable.

This love is that salt that seasoneth our harsh and dull labours, and gives a pleasant relish to our other unsavoury proceedings; when love goes, the shadows gather, old age with its stiff joints, disease, &c. All our feasts almost, masques, mummings, banquets, merry meetings, weddings, pleasing songs, fine tunes, Poems, Love-stories, Plays, Comedies . . . &c., proceed hence.[18]

Take away love "and take all pleasure, joy, comfort, happiness and true content out of the world."

In its sexual manifestations it is a "stubborn and unbridled passion," not to be denied without serious consequences. If it be not "eased or amended, it breaks out often into outrageous and prodigious events." Men infatuated "forget all honesty, shame and common civility . . . become senseless and mad . . . no better than beasts, irrational, stupid, headstrong, void of fear of God or men, they frequently forswear themselves, spend, steal, commit

---

[17] *Ibid.*, p. 740.   [18] *Ibid.*, pp. 758–759.

incests, rapes, adulteries, murders, depopulate Towns, Cities, Countries, to satisfy their lust." [19]

It is, therefore,

odious and abominable . . . to lead a single life against the laws of nature, opposite to religion, policy, and humanity, so to starve, to offer violence to, to suppress the vigour of youth! by rigorous statutes, severe laws, vain persuasions, to debar them of that to which by their innate temperature [constitution] they are so furiously inclined, urgently carried, and sometimes precipitated, even irresistibly led, to the prejudice of their soul's health, and good estate of body and mind! [20]

He protests angrily against the celibacy which was then required of academics: "It is an unnatural and impious thing" to prohibit "Christian liberty" in these matters. "Fearful maladies," not to mention "gross inconveniences," come upon both sexes as a result of enforced sexual abstinence. It is inhuman, and from it proceeds "many diseases, many vices, mastupration, satyriasis, priapism, melancholy, madness, fornication, adultery, buggary, sodomy, theft, murder, and all manner of mischiefs." [21]

He recognized the perversions as consequences of frustrated love, but was inclined to regard them as substitute gratifications, resorted to because of the denial of opportunities for normal satisfaction. He seemed to think, that is, that perverts would be normal if they possessed, at the moment of their act, normal opportunities for gratification.

From frustrated love, he maintained, comes fear and sorrow, desperation and fury. For love and hatred are inseparable: "These concupiscible and irascible appetites are as the two twists of a rope, mutually mixed one with the other, and both twining about the heart." The unloved are full of "biting cares, perturbations, passions, sorrows, fears, suspicions, discontents, discords, wars, treacheries, enmities, flattery . . . lust, impudence [and] cruelty."

Jealousy is "the child of insatiate love," and the jealous man, tormenting himself with his own fears, restless, irrational, agonizingly insecure, is the very epitome of madness:

[19] *Ibid.*, pp. 762–763.   [20] *Ibid.*, p. 356.   [21] *Ibid.*, pp. 810–811.

Jealousy . . . begets unquietness in the mind night and day . . . he misinterprets every thing is said or done, most apt to mistake or misconster . . . 'Tis proper to Jealousy so to do,

> *Pale hag, infernal fury, pleasure's smart,*
> *Envy's observer, prying into every part.*   (DANIEL)

Besides those strange gestures of staring, frowning, grinning, rolling of eyes, menacing, ghastly looks, broken pace, interrupt, precipitate, half-turns. He will sometimes sigh, weep, sob for anger,

> *Such thunder-storms in sooth pour down their showers,*

swear and belie, slander any man, curse, threaten, brawl, scold, fight; and sometimes again flatter, and speak fair, ask forgiveness, kiss and coll, condemn his rashness and folly, vow, protest and swear he will never do so again; and then eftsoons, impatient as he is, rave, roar, and lay about him like a madman, thump her sides, drag her about perchance, drive her out of doors, send her home, he will be divorced forthwith, she is a whore, &c., by and by with all submiss compliment intreat her fair, and bring her in again, he loves her dearly, she is his sweet, most kind, and loving wife, he will not change, not leave her for a Kingdom; so he continues off and on, as the toy [trifle] takes him, the object moves him, but most part brawling, fretting, unquiet he is, accusing and suspecting not strangers only, but Brothers and Sisters, Father and Mother, nearest and dearest friends. . . . And through fear conceives unto himself things almost incredible and impossible to be effected. As an Heron when she fishes, still prying on all sides, or as a Cat doth a Mouse, his eye is never off hers; he gloats on him, on her, accurately observing on whom she looks, who looks at her, what she saith, doth, at dinner, at supper, sitting, walking, at home, abroad, he is the same, still inquiring, mandering, gazing, listening, affrighted with every small object; why did she smile, why did she pity him, commend him? why did she drink twice to such a man? why did she offer to kiss, to dance? &c., a whore, a whore, an arrant whore! [22]

Some people seek to avoid disappointment in love by centering their affections wholly upon themselves. But the self, Burton perceived, is not a satisfactory love object, and self-love leads invariably to melancholy: it is "a great assault and cause," a "violent batterer of our souls." For as the lover seeks to exalt his mistress

[22] *Ibid.*, pp. 840–841.

beyond all rational limits, so the lover of self seeks to exalt himself. And

> those men which have no other object of their Love than greatness, wealth, authority, &c., are rather feared than beloved; they neither loved nor are loved; and howsoever borne with for a time, yet for their tyranny and oppression, griping, covetousness, currish hardness, folly, intemperance, imprudence, and such like vices, they are generally odious, abhorred of all.[23]

Covetousness—irrational, insatiate desire, based on eternal insecurity—is their dominant characteristic. They are rash and usually wretched.

In a way, Burton maintains, self-love might be regarded as the fountainhead of all melancholy. For love of self prevents the love of others. Unloving, the man feels unloved; and unloved, insecure. Insecurity breeds fear, and fear, preying upon the mind, distorts the imagination "which, misinforming the heart, causeth all these distemperatures."

There seem to be so many fountainheads! The trouble, as Burton was fully aware, was to decide which, if any, was a main cause and which were secondary and contributory causes.

The plain, if not the main, cause was undeniably this same "distorted imagination." On that point, fundamental to his etiology, Burton was, apparently, willing to rely on his own intuition, his "melancholizing," as he called it, in opposition to the learned authors toward whom in so much else he was compliant. He recognized, indeed, that certain physical difficulties seemed to accompany melancholy, but these, he maintained, were effects. For the imagination, stimulating the emotions wrongly, especially the emotion of fear, could cause "alteration and confusion of spirits and humours; by means of which, so disturbed, concoction is hindered, and the principal parts are much debilitated."

Therefore, "great is the force of imagination, and much more ought the cause of melancholy to be ascribed to this alone, than to the distemperature of the body."[24]

[23] *Ibid.*, p. 634.   [24] *Ibid.*, p. 219.

The ultimate cause of melancholy, then, would be whatever distorts the imagination in this particular way. And this, Burton believed, was uncontrolled desire, the "concupiscible" and "irascible" appetites, which, "drowned in the organs of sense," that is to say latent in the animal, non-"human" part of us, lay beyond the reach of reason.

Those most susceptible to this lack of emotional stability were those with a hereditary tendency toward it. And aggravating this were the denial of affection in childhood and the deflection of the sexual impulse from its proper channels.

Lastly, supplementing and, it may be, including all these, is another cause—the maladjustment of the individual to society or, conversely—as Burton's temperament led him to view it—the maladjustment of society to the individual.

Therapy

For a disease springing from so many, so varied, such deep-rooted and inter-reacting causes there could hardly be a single, simple cure, for "mixt diseases," as Burton said in discussing this very point, "must have mixt remedies."

For some forms of mental disturbance he felt that there was small hope of any betterment; little, if anything, so far as he knew, could be done for epilepsy, for example, or for apoplexy, or "dotage" (senile dementia) or "inveterate melancholy" (psychoses).

Other forms of depression, particularly those resulting from some temporary physical condition, such as jaundice, amenorrhea, or "suppression of hemrods," offered a favorable prognosis of complete, and often speedy, cure.

True melancholy lay somewhere between these two groups. Something could be done for it. It might be "mitigated and much eased." But it was rarely completely eradicated; it generally "accompanied to the grave" those who were afflicted with it.

In discussing treatment, as in discussing causes, Burton is restricted by the conceptions of his age. Thus, he feels obliged to list a whole series of "unlawful" cures, cures that depended on magic, witchcraft, charms, and exorcisms and hence were "not to be tolerated or endured," since they jeopardized the soul.

Certain other remedies, like certain causes, were time-honored and so had to be reviewed in an "anatomy," even though he was obviously not enthusiastic about them. Toward the science of phlebotomy, for instance, for all its dominance of current practice, he is decidedly cool and toward one of its major treatments for melancholy—the application of horse leeches to hemorrhoids—

he is positively chilly, though this may be but one more example of the manner in which his personal experiences shaped his theory.

He had read that some successes had been achieved by trepanning, and the novelty of it seemed to appeal to his whimsical mind: " 'tis not amiss to bore the skull with an instrument, to let out the fuliginous vapors"; though he agrees with Gordonius that this treatment had best be reserved as a last resort.

Some of the other remedies that he lists seem to be based on sympathetic magic. Thus, the anointing of the face with hare's blood as a cure for excessive blushing would appear to be connected with the popular belief that the hare was the most timid of all animals. The rubbing of the soles of the feet with the fat of a dormouse probably owed its reputation as a cure for insomnia to the creature's habit of hibernation.[1] If anxiety could be caused—as certain learned authors asserted that it could—by wearing a garment made from the wool of a sheep that had been worried by a wolf, then it could be cured by removing all such garments from the patient's wardrobe; and so forth.

The absurdity of such cures stamps them strongly on our minds, but the striking thing, actually, is how small a part they play in Burton's discussion of treatment. Equally striking is what is omitted. One of the commonest popular theories for the treatment of the "possessed," for example, held that the demon could be forced out of possession if the patient could be made to swallow substances so grossly revolting that the demon could not endure them. Particular prescriptions intended to effect this sort of cure are nauseating beyond belief, and it is significant that despite their widespread use Burton hardly alludes to them. He may well have regarded them as beneath serious consideration, but there is reason to believe that he was repelled by their barbarity. For his approach to his subject is marked by deep humanity and sympathy. He laughs, to be sure, at some of the antics of the melancholy, but it is not a derisive laughter; he never forgets that, in spite of their

[1] It is not so clear why "the ear wax of a dog" should act as a soporific when rubbed on the teeth. "Scarcely possible to believe," says Burton in a footnote.

occasional ludicrousness, they are men and women in excruciating pain and misery.

When one bears in mind the dreadful treatment then—and for centuries thereafter—given to the insane in public institutions, Burton's compassion looms very large. There is no darker chapter in the whole ghastly chronicle of man's inhumanity to man than the suffering that was formerly inflicted on the mentally sick. They were flogged and starved, chained in filthy, unheated kennels, naked and unclean, objects, not of pity, but of amusement and derision. To visit Bedlam and other asylums in order to goad and bait the unhappy inmates was a popular diversion. There was a regular charge for admission. Family picnics were encouraged, and, lest brutality be limited by ignorance, there were special guides who for a slight tip would indicate which of the wretched patients would display the most interesting resentment if poked with a stick or asked certain questions.[2]

At a time when such callous cruelty was taken for granted, Burton insisted that the melancholy and the psychotic were *more* sensitive to slights and *more* alive to suffering than normal people and should, therefore, be treated with the most delicate consideration. He goes beyond even a great deal of twentieth-century practice in this, protesting with fervor, for example, against the unfeeling heartiness with which so many well-meaning but obtuse physicians drive neurotics into exasperation or despair. It is of no use whatever, he insists repeatedly, to tell the melancholy man to cheer up. It is not only a waste of time to try to show him that his fears are groundless, but it adds to his distress; he feels more helpless than ever at the thought that not even the physician understands. "You may as well bid him that is diseased not to feel pain, as a melancholy man not to fear, not to be sad: 'tis within his blood, his brains, his whole temperature [composition]; it cannot be removed."[3]

He does not feel, though, that the situation is hopeless. The pa-

<hr/>

[2] For one illustration see Ned Ward, *The London Spy*, first published in book form London, 1703; [new ed.], London, 1927, pp. 51–55.
[3] *Anatomy*, p. 470.

tient may "in some sort correct himself." He may choose whether he will give way too far to his own morbid tendencies. But *he* must choose. The exhortations of an outsider are better omitted.

The number of treatments and "cures" that Burton examines is tremendous. Something seemed to compel him to describe every remedy listed in the approved authorities, and his impetuous nature led him to discuss each cure with a zest that convinces the reader that here, at last, is *the* cure, the one remedy that the *Anatomy* endorses. But the next is presented with equal enthusiasm, and the next and the next. And each in turn, after a great array of authorities and cases has been reviewed, is dismissed as uncertain, imperfect, and unproven.

He arrives at the general conclusion that there is no specific remedy, no catholic medicine for this sickness. It is an individual matter; that which helps one man may be pernicious to another. And in no case is there an abrupt cure; all must be "by art and insinuation."

Purgatives—both "upwards" and "downwards," as emetics and laxatives were formerly designated—were the commonest of all medicines then prescribed for melancholy. The theory was that the patient was "out of humour"—that is, was suffering from an imbalance of one of the four humors, blood, phlegm, bile, and black bile or melancholy (to use its Greek name), whose mixture in due proportion (temper) constituted the basis of health. Obviously the purging of the excess humor was indicated, and every case, if we may judge from the prescriptions, was felt to require vigorous treatment. "Fitter for a horse than a man," Burton grumbles, after describing several famous prescriptions, and, indeed, they were! White hellebore, for instance, "a strong purger upward," was prescribed by those who believed in firm measures and no nonsense. But even its warmest advocates had to confess that its action was so violent that it ought not to be administered to "old men, youths . . . [or] such as fear strangling." Burton says that to his horror he had heard market folk ask for it in an apothecary's shop "by pennyworths, and such irrational ways." And he doubts not but that they went home and swallowed it: "but with what success

God knows; they smart often for their rash boldness and folly, break a vein, make their eyes ready to start out of their heads, or kill themselves." [4]

For himself, he will give no prescriptions, at least not in English, lest he thereby "give occasion to some ignorant reader to practice on himself." But he had a deeper reason: he didn't believe that medicines did much good. Despite all the great authorities, "common experience" had shown that "they live freest from all manner of infirmities that make the least use of apothecary's physic." Physicians kill as many as they save, and the most famous prescriptions are often "fopperies and fictions."

On certain mild stimulants and narcotics, substances which were then felt to be medicinal, but are now a part of the daily diet of every household, he was inclined to look with more favor. A "decoction of china roots," [5] he affirms, "makes a good color in the face, takes away melancholy and all infirmities proceeding from cold"—though it is plain that he is using "melancholy" here in its lighter, "improper" sense. Sassafras and sarsaparilla make cheering beverages, and he has read that the Turks derive great solace from a drink called coffee, made from a berry "as black as soot, and as bitter," which they "sip of, and sup as warm as they can suffer."

They spend much time [travellers report], in those Coffee-houses, which are somewhat like our Aiehouses or Taverns, and there they sit chatting and drinking to drive away the time, and to be merry together, because they find by experience that kind of drink so used helpeth digestion and procureth alacrity.[6]

Wine, he feels, is good in moderation, and beer is "a most wholesome and pleasant drink." Though a teetotaler himself, he doubts that even an excess of alcohol does as much harm as some would have us think, quoting Rabelais's observation that there are more old drunkards than old physicians.

Tobacco, "divine, rare, superexcellent Tobacco," is "a sovereign remedy" if not used to excess, beyond all "panaceas, potable gold, and philosopher's stones."

[4] *Ibid.*, pp. 575–576.   [5] Tea.   [6] *Ibid.*, p. 593.

A good vomit, I confess, a virtuous herb, if it be well qualified, opportunely taken, and medicinally used, but, as it is commonly abused by most men, which take it as Tinkers do Ale, 'tis a plague, a mischief, a violent purger of goods, land, health, hellish, devilish, and damned Tobacco, the ruin and overthrow of body and soul.[7]

If the praise of the first part of this comment seems excessive, it must be remembered that almost magic properties were ascribed to tobacco when it was introduced. And if the condemnation of the last part seems excessive, it must be remembered that the author of *A Counterblaste to Tobacco* then sat on the English throne, and that an unqualified rebuttal of a royal opinion was more unsalutary than tobacco ever could be.

But aside from recommending a few such mild lenitives, the discreet physician, Burton felt, would rely chiefly on "kitchen physic" or diet. And there no rules could be laid down, for ultimately a man's own experience of what does and what does not agree with him must be his guide: "Tiberius in Tacitus did laugh at all such, that after 30 years of age would ask counsel of others concerning matters of diet; I say the same." [8]

Nonetheless, he fills scores of pages with lists of the various foods that at one time or another have been forbidden to the melancholy by this or that author, until finally almost everything ever eaten by man has been interdicted, and he admits, with a smile, that he has "put most men out of commons." But it is evident that it doesn't matter, because he did not expect any reader to take him very seriously in this regard. The important thing, as he sees it, in the diet of the melancholy is temperance. Moderation is more to the point than any particular choice or restriction—especially since gluttony is so frequently a fault with them. A melancholy man, he warns, "had better put water in his shoes" than overeat or overdrink.

Abstinence and fasting are as bad as overeating and overdrinking. What the melancholy patient needs is a light but sufficient diet of foods that experience has shown him are not indigestible. For his problem in diet is, not to find some food that will cure him or to avoid some one food that is causing his sickness, but rather to

[7] *Ibid.*, p. 577.   [8] *Ibid.*, p. 402.

avoid digestive disturbances that are so often contributory factors to his periods of depression.

In fact, one of the chief objectives in the treatment of melancholy must be to avoid, so far as possible, *all* conditions and situations that tend to excite it. And chief among these, Burton felt, were solitude and idleness, conditions that were to be sedulously avoided. The patient or his physician must plan a regime of continual occupation among pleasant company and congenial surroundings. Travel is excellent, not so much for the change of air, for which so many medical writers recommend it, but because of the diversion it supplies: "No better Physick for a melancholy man than change of air and variety of places, to travel abroad and see fashions." Nothing so effective to arouse the mind from its lethargy as new sights and new customs; besides, the old haunts have associations that continually put the patient in mind of his woes.

Since it isn't the change of air, primarily, or the mere moving from one place to another, but the diversion that it offers that makes traveling effective, those who cannot afford it need not despair, for there are many cheaper ways, within the reach of all, to lure the melancholy from their continual and morbid self-preoccupation. Anything that "sets the mind awork and distracts cogitations" will do. Best of all is "continual business," something that fills the mind, without exciting or irritating it. The melancholy man *must* have a settled occupation, and it must be something that seems worth while to him. "No better cure . . . than to have some employment or other." [9]

It is well, perhaps, to learn some art or science, for studies often serve to distract the troubled mind. But they are dangerous; sometimes they increase rather than diminish melancholy. Reading is too solitary and sedentary, and, as the Preacher said, he that increases knowledge increases sorrow. Burton seemed to think that his own melancholy was in part the consequence of too much study. Yet, to occupy his mind and to keep from brooding, he studied still more, thus making "an antidote of the prime cause of the disease."

[9] *Ibid.*, p. 440.

The best diversion is one that exercises mind and body, "not one, but both, and that in a mediocrity [moderation]." Sports are good if the patient is not too contemptuous of them or, on the other hand, does not enter into them with harmful violence, for many men "will voluntarily undertake that, to satisfy their pleasure, which a poor man for a good stipend would scarce be hired to undergo." Among sports, by the way, Burton particularly commends fly-fishing: its "variety of Baits for all seasons, and pretty devices" occupy the mind without stimulating it too much, and even if the fisherman catches nothing, he has a pleasant walk and a quiet pastime out of doors.[10]

Games are good, but the melancholy are inclined to take all contests too seriously. They are over eager to win and do not, as a rule, accept defeat gracefully; so that there is the danger that games which divert and relax others may serve only to agitate them more deeply. Chess, for instance, "is a good and witty exercise of the mind . . . but if it proceed from overmuch study . . . it may do more harm than good; it is a game too troublesome for some men's brains, too full of anxiety, all out as bad as study; besides it is a testy, cholerick game, and very offensive to him that loseth the Mate." [11]

Playing for stakes is worse than not playing at all, because it excites anger, covetousness, and resentment. Furthermore, it may lead to losses which the melancholy temperament will exaggerate into calamities or even, of course, to losses which would justify depression in the most rational minds.

Solitude is as bad as idleness. "Be not solitary, be not idle" is Burton's parting precept. Dr. Johnson, who approved, though he did not always heed, this warning, believed that it was the combination that Burton felt should be avoided: he paraphrased the famous injunction to mean, "If you are solitary, do not be idle; if you are idle, do not be alone."

Burton makes it quite plain, though, that the mere presence of other people does not suffice to remove solitude. They must be companionable people, acceptable to the patient, "friends and

[10] *Ibid.*, pp. 442–443.   [11] *Ibid.*, p. 450.

familiars" who can imperceptibly draw him from his moody thoughts.

Everything possible must be done to dispel the patient's feeling of being rejected or despised. In contrast to the filthy state in which so many of the mentally afflicted were then allowed to languish, Burton urged that the melancholy man should be "neatly dressed, washed, and combed, according to his ability at least, in clean sweet linen, spruce, handsome, decent [comely], and good apparel; for nothing sooner dejects a man than want, squalor, nastiness, foul or old cloaths out of fashion." Despite their dispirited tendency to disregard their own appearance, the melancholy must be kept unusually clean; for dirtiness is depressing—it "dulleth the spirits." [12]

In addition the patient should have "mirth and merry company," and since "Venus doth many of them much good," those whose depression can be traced to abstinence should not remain celibate. The "last refuge and surest remedy" of love melancholy is "to let them go together." Aesculapius himself could prescribe nothing better. Moody virgins should get them husbands betimes, and melancholy maids and widows must be "well placed and married to good husbands in due time; that's the primary cause and this the ready cure." Sex is often the best sedative: "if she be not satisfied, you know where and when, nothing but quarrels, all is in an uproar, and there is little quietness to be had." [13]

But medicines or surgery, change of air, moderation in diet, a pleasing occupation, sexual gratification—none of these things, nor all of them together, will suffice. They attack only the periphery of the trouble. For if the basic cause is, as Burton saw it to be, "imagination misinforming the heart," then the basic cure must include some means of controlling the errant imagination. The heart must no longer be misinformed. That is to say, the body and the mind must be freed from the tyranny of passions which, springing as they do from an emotional distortion, can find no adequate expression or release: "Whosoever he is that shall hope to cure this malady in himself or any other, must first rectify these passions and

[12] *Ibid.*, pp. 583–584, 403. [13] *Ibid.*, p. 793.

perturbations of the mind; the chiefest cure consists in them." [14]

How is that to be done, however? The sufferer is certainly not able to rectify his own passions and perturbations; indeed, one of his greatest difficulties is that he does not recognize the distortions in his mind, does not, usually, even suspect their presence. He is often the complete and tragic dupe of his own self-justifications.

The first essential, therefore, is some external fixed point of reference from which he may estimate the degree of his imagination's distortion. And that, of course, can only be another person, some particular friend to whom he may "open himself" of his grief. Experience has shown that nothing else is "so forcible to strengthen, recreate and heal the wounded soul of a miserable man." "Opportunity of speech" is the "true Nepenthes" for the sorrows of melancholy. [15]

If then our judgement be so depraved, our reason over-ruled, will precipitated, that we cannot seek our own good, or moderate ourselves, as in this disease commonly it is, the best way for ease is to impart our misery to some friend, not to smother it up in our own breast; canker thrives and flourishes by concealment, &c., and that which was most offensive to us, a cause of fear and grief, another hell; for grief concealed strangles the soul; but when as we shall but impart it to some discreet, trusty, loving friend, it is instantly removed, by his counsel haply, wisdom, persuasion, advice, his good means, which we could not otherwise apply unto ourselves. . . . The simple narration many times easeth our distressed mind, & in the midst of greatest extremities; so divers have been relieved, by exonerating [unburdening] themselves to a faithful friend: he sees that which we cannot see for passion and discontent. [16]

Many of the melancholy, of course, cannot reveal the true cause of their grief and fear because they do not themselves "discern what is amiss." They are self-deceived. The best of advice may seem bad or irrelevant to them, or they may be so helpless in the grip of their misery that they cannot act at all. "Most men in this malady are spiritually sick, void of reason almost, over-borne by

[14] *Ibid.*, p. 467.   [15] *Ibid.*, p. 476.   [16] *Ibid.*, pp. 471–472.

their miseries, and too deep an apprehension of their sins, they cannot apply themselves to good counsel." [17]

In these cases it is the friend's first duty to discover, if he can, the true cause of the perturbation. He must look behind the offered explanation, however sincerely it is offered, seeking in the patient's "looks, gestures, motions [and] phantasy" to find a clew that will lead him to the real explanation.[18] Nor need he expect the sick man to accept the truth, once it has been perceived. Melancholy is rarely recognized as such until it has continued long and is deeply ingrained in the whole personality of the sufferer. It is not to be eradicated at once. The treatment will be long, even at the best, and at first the friend must be content "to remove all objects, causes, companies, occasions, as may anyways molest him, to humour him, please him, divert him, and, if it be possible, by altering his course of life, to give him security and satisfaction." [19]

It is obvious that the obligations which the friend assumes are heavy, and it is equally obvious that he must have wide learning and unusual talents. For one thing, he must have a knowledge of medicine. Many of the secondary causes and complications of the disease are physical, and only a physician can treat them. And, in addition, the physician has another advantage to fit him for the role of confessor: his profession invests him with a certain authority, and it is most important that the patient choose as his confidant one whom he respects—one, even, of whom he stands a little in awe. For the friend, as has been said, must be the fixed point of reference from which the patient is ultimately to become aware of his own aberration, and his whole value, from this point of view, depends on the patient's conviction that he *is* fixed, steadfast, and immovable; and this he is not likely to feel, in times of stress, when he needs to feel it most, except concerning one whom he regards with great respect.[20]

Merely being a physician, however, does not qualify a man to assist the melancholy by receiving their confessions. It is plain that

[17] *Ibid.*, p. 951.

[18] *Ibid.*, p. 473; "motions" means impulses, particularly sexual impulses (see p. 107n); "phantasy" means imaginings in general.

[19] *Ibid.*, p. 473.   [20] *Ibid.*, pp. 389, 778.

there should be, in addition to a general knowledge of medicine, a particular knowledge of melancholy. A still further requirement, and not the least by any means, is that the physician-friend should have first searched his own heart and made sure that *it* is not misinformed by a distorted imagination. Only to "a prepared bosom" can the melancholy profitably confide their troubles. The physician who desires to help them must first rectify the passions and perturbations of his own mind, so that he may not mislead them and so that he may endure with patience and equanimity their emotional vagaries.[21]

For melancholy persons are "more troublesome to their physicians than ordinary patients." They are "averse, peevish, waspish." They exaggerate their symptoms, eternally demand attention, continually desire some new form of treatment. They are filled with a succession of superficial hopes, and when these fail of fulfillment, as they almost always do, the patient turns on his physician. Resentment and suspicion are symptoms of their disease, and the physician may often find himself the victim of their violence and unreasonableness.[22]

He must be prepared for this, and prepared to endure it with good humor. To become angry would be to frustrate all therapy; the physician who allows himself to lose his temper when dealing with a melancholy patient is madder than the patient. One forgetful moment, one outburst of exasperation, can undo the work of months or years. For the melancholy are not rational; despite the aggressiveness of their own temperaments, they do not permit aggression from others. The physician who forgets himself and strikes back may lose the patient's confidence, and confidence, in this relationship, comes "before art, precepts, and all remedies whatsoever." "An Empirick oftentimes, and a silly Chirurgeon, doth more strange cures than a rational Physician" if he have the patient's full confidence. " 'Tis opinion alone (saith Cardan) that makes or mars Physicians, and he doth the best cures, according to Hippocrates, in whom most trust." [23]

This, the personal influence of the physician over the patient,

[21] *Ibid.*, p. 472.   [22] *Ibid.*, p. 392.   [23] *Ibid.*, p. 223.

is the "notable secret" of the successes that have been achieved in the care of this sickness. The purgings, the bleedings, and the exorcisms have only been, at the best, accessories.

Many do not come under the care of a physician until they are already advanced into a state of despair, and with these the first necessity is the arousing of a desire to be cured. Without that there is no hope. In other maladies, "above all things whatsoever we desire help & health, a present [immediate] recovery, if by any means possible it may be procured." [24] But to the melancholy man "nothing so tedious, nothing so odious"; the life which other men seek to preserve he abhors. Through easement of the worst of his physical complications, through mild diversion and pleasant company, and, above all, through his interest in the physician, the patient must be brought to *desire* health. "We must live by faith," Burton says, transposing the wisdom of theology to a secular use, and " 'tis the beginning of grace to wish for grace." [25]

And as a sign of grace the patient must be willing to make sacrifices. He must not be "too niggardly miserable of his purse," for one thing. Such counsel would certainly be open to cynical interpretation if it came from a physician, but coming from Burton who, on the whole, is inclined to be a little resentful of the "purse-milking tribe," as he calls them, it is striking. It is plain that he meant that the patient must be genuinely desirous of being cured, that he must sincerely place the wish for health before all other considerations. The treatment cannot hope to be successful if it is merely a subterfuge on the part of the patient.

What, then, is needed, as Burton sees it, in the care of melancholy, is a physician who has knowledge, self-control, and self-knowledge, assurance and honesty. If he is to interpret the patient's "looks, gestures, motions [and] phantasy," he must also, one assumes, possess imaginative intelligence. Certain qualities are required in the patient, also, if there is to be any hope of cure: he must have obedience, constancy, a true desire to be healed, and submission to and confidence in the physician.

Granted the combination of a physician and patient with these

[24] *Ibid.*, p. 370.   [25] *Ibid.*, p. 967.

qualities, respectively—and granted, furthermore, that the patient is not epileptic, apoplectic, completely insane, or senile—the prognosis, as Burton sees it, is not wholly dark. He is wisely cautious, however, and will promise no wonders. A complete cure, in the sense that one speaks of a cure of smallpox or of a broken leg, is rarely achieved, but with good luck, he insists, a certain number of patients do improve sufficiently to be able to live again among their fellow men on terms of equality.

To the inexperienced layman this may seem a most lame and impotent conclusion. But to Burton, who knew the difficulties and complexities of treatment and, above all, the helplessness of the un-aided neurotic, it was a great achievement: "Believe Robert, who speaketh from experience. Something I can speak out of experience, painful experience hath taught me."[26]

And difficult and imperfect as the cure may be, it is almost easy and complete compared to prevention. For while the cure has to deal only with the vagaries and difficulties of the single individual, prevention must deal with the infinite intricacies and conflicting forces of all society. For the troubles of the neurotic, more often than not, have their origin in his social background, in circumstances beyond his control and usually beyond his comprehension.

In his discussion of symptoms Burton had suggested, almost off-hand, that melancholy itself might be a symptom—a symptom of sickness in society. As he proceeded with his work, this apparently casual idea seemed to assume more and more importance in his mind, until, by the time he had finished, it had become one of his dominant thoughts and led him, as a summing up of the whole matter, to propose, in his address to the reader, a remodeling of the whole of society in the interests of mental hygiene.

There are many references throughout the *Anatomy* to the relation existing between mental disturbances and the structure of society, and these, when brought together with the long section on the subject in his introduction, constitute an impressive discussion of culture and neurosis.

[26] *Ibid.*, p. 17.

He commences by noting the brutally aggressive and competitive nature of European society and the miseries that ensue from that fact:

The greatest enemy to man is man . . . no fiend can so torment, insult over, tyrannize, vex, as one man doth another . . . earthquakes, inundations, ruins of houses, consuming fires, come by little and little, or make some noise before-hand; but the knaveries, impostures, injuries, and villainies, of men no art can avoid.[27]

Men prey upon one another, he observes, like ravenous beasts. One must kill or be killed. Force and cunning are combined against every defenseless man. The organization of society which seems to offer protection is actually an instrument of exploitation directed by the strong against the weak. On every hand there is rapine and injustice. The man who makes shoes goes barefoot. They who harvest the crops are sick for lack of food. The producers of wealth have nothing. A poor man is hanged for stealing a sheep, though driven to the theft by necessity of "intolerable cold, hunger & thirst, to save himself from starving"; but a great man in office may rob whole provinces in complete security, ruin thousands, and finally "be recompensed with turgent titles, honoured for his good service, and no man dare to find fault, or mutter at it." As the final touch, indeed, the great thief is sometimes made a judge and from the bench condemns the little thief.[28]

In each estate there is no heart's rest.

Children live in a perpetual slavery, still under that tyrannical government of masters: young men, and of riper years, subject to labour, and a thousand cares of the world, to treachery, falsehood, and cozenage [cheating] . . . [the] old are full of aches in their bones, cramps and convulsions, earth-bent, dull of hearing, weak-sighted, hoary, wrinkled, harsh, so much altered as that they cannot know their own face in a glass, a burden to themselves and others; after 70 years, *all is sorrow* (as David hath it), they do not live but linger. If they be sound, they fear diseases; if sick, weary of their lives: Long years are not life; healthy years are life. One complains of want, a second of servitude, another of a secret or incurable disease, of some deformity of body, of

[27] *Ibid.*, p. 117.   [28] *Ibid.*, pp. 50-54.

some loss, danger, death of friends, shipwreck, persecution, imprisonment, disgrace, repulse, contumely, calumny, abuse, injury, contempt,
ingratitude, unkindness, scoffs, flouts, unfortunate marriage, single life,
too many children, no children, unhappy children, barrenness, false
servants, banishment, oppression, frustrate hopes, and ill success, &c.[29]

Their souls are crucified, their bodies are withered, riveled up
like old apples, their days are cumbersome, slow and dull.

Men spend their lives in toil in order to be gentry, "yet the badge
of gentry is idleness." The rich are drones, consuming the fruits
of others' labor in vicious boredom.

And thence it comes to pass that in City and Country so many griev-
ances of body and mind, and this feral disease of Melancholy so frequently rageth, and now domineers almost all over Europe amongst
our great ones. They know not how to spend their time (disports
excepted, which are all their business), what to do, or otherwise how to
bestow themselves. . . . Every man almost hath something or other
to employ himself about, some vocation, some trade, but they do all by
ministers and servants; they consider themselves born for ease, when
truly it is often to their own and others' detriment.[30]

The poor are slaves and captives, working "day and night in
coal-pits, tin-mines, with sore toil to maintain a poor living . . .
in extreme anguish, and pain." [31] They are usually paralyzed by
superstition and bound by ignorance. Every generation sees millions of them killed in wars of which they have no understanding
and from which they can hope to gain nothing, not even fame: out
of "fifteen thousand proletaries slain in battle, scarce fifteen are
recorded in history, or one alone, the general perhaps, and after a
while his & their names are likewise blotted out, the whole battle
itself is forgotten."

If some poor man does have some talent or capacity for thought,
and if he is endowed with the extra energy needed to make some
display of it in addition to performing his daily drudgery, and if
by some accident he finds the time and manages to bring himself
to the attention of those who can appreciate and perhaps reward
him, it is more likely to bring him added misery and despair than

[29] *Ibid.*, pp. 241–242.   [30] *Ibid.*, pp. 439–440.   [31] *Ibid.*, p. 495.

to do him any good.[32] For the poor are trapped in their own misfortunes. Abilities and merits which in another sphere would be highly prized are despised in them because of their poverty.

The road to virtue is obstructed by poverty, 'tis hard for a poor man to rise, they do not easily rise, whose narrow fortunes stand in the way of their merits; the wisdom of the poor is despised, and his words are not heard, his works are rejected, contemned, for the baseness and obscurity of the author; though laudable and good in themselves, they will not likely take.[33]

In a world in which "all sorts, sects, ages and conditions are thus out of tune," what need is there, Burton demands, to seek for the causes of melancholy in such trifles as constipation or the spells of witches? "Were there no other particular affliction," he says bitterly, "to molest a man in this life, the very cogitation of that common misery were enough to macerate, and make him weary of his life; to think that he can never be secure, but still in danger, sorrow, grief, and persecution." [34]

The cure of individuals can at the best be only a palliative measure. If we are to get at the roots of melancholy, all human society must be fundamentally reorganized: "The whole world belike should be new moulded . . . & turned inside out, as we do haycocks in Harvest, top to bottom, or bottom to top." [35]

To show what he meant, Burton sketched a utopian commonwealth in which reforms would have removed the frustrations that he felt contributed so largely to the formation of the neurotic personality in his own day; it was to be a world in which it would not be necessary to "bangle away our best days, befool out our times," and "lead a contentious, discontent, tumultuous, melancholy, miserable life." It is an extraordinary document, and deserves more attention than it has received in the histories of such writings.

Like all utopias, it is a reformed version of the author's own

---

[32] More than two hundred and fifty years later Thomas Hardy shocked and angered his own generation by stating the same idea in *Jude the Obscure*. See also the 166th *Rambler*, by Samuel Johnson.

[33] *Anatomy*, p. 303.   [34] *Ibid.*, pp. 235–236.   [35] *Ibid.*, p. 412.

society, but the nature of the particular reforms that Burton advocates is most interesting from a psychiatric point of view.

To remove the exasperation of economic inequality, he would have all property controlled and profits limited in the public interest. He would have a state bank to direct finance and a department of agriculture to regulate planting, harvesting, and erosion—"because private possessors are many times idiots." The inheritance of property is to be permitted, but any property employed against the public weal is to be confiscated.

The laws are to be revised with a view to preventing instead of punishing crime, "for many punishments are not less a disgrace to the governor than many funerals to a physician." All customs (except inheritance) that perpetuate privilege are to be abolished. Like all other designers of utopias, he would lessen the number of lawyers. The government of his ideal society is to be administered by a trained bureaucracy, admission to which, as to all offices in the land, is to be through a civil service examination.

Wages and hours are to be regulated by the state in the interest of the workers. He has a form of price control and a vast program of public works to ensure stabilization of wages and continual employment. Hospitals, health insurance, and old age pensions are to lift some of the burden of fear from the poor.

Scientific research is to be supported by the state, and ideas are to be judged on their merits, not on the social position of those who conceive them. The public laboratories are to be the apex of a vast system of free public education, which, by making for equality of opportunity, are to be one of the chief means of removing the favoritism and special privilege that so corrupted and poisoned seventeenth-century England. In the public schools, by the way, languages are "not to be taught by those tedious precepts ordinarily used, but by use, example, conversation, as travellers learn abroad, & nurses teach their children." [36]

The responsibilities and duties of municipal government he will have taken over by the educated and intelligent. Then, as now,

[36] *Ibid.*, p. 84.

city offices seem to have passed by default into the hands of the ignorant and the corrupt, and Burton felt strongly that something must be done to change this if life were to be more tolerable for the common citizen. Among other civic improvements he lists sanitary laws, with special officers to enforce them, supervision of markets, zoning, municipal housing projects, and the elimination of slums.[37]

"Only such parents as are sound of mind and body should be suffered to marry." Those with "some enormous hereditary disease of body or mind" are to be prohibited from marrying, although "other order shall be taken for their content." Burton will not go so far as to urge that all males carrying hereditary diseases should be castrated and all females incarcerated for life, but the desirability of such stringent measures is "more to be looked into than it is." The assumption that marriage is a wholly private affair had resulted, he felt, in "a vast confusion of hereditary diseases." The race was becoming biologically corrupt as those weak in mind and body multiplied apace. Insanity, especially, was spreading unchecked, many a poisoned root infecting whole families: "our fathers bad, and we are like to be worse." [38]

His eugenics does not stop with the prohibition of marriage to the unfit; it required marriage of all the fit, of all men at twenty-five and all women at twenty. Dowers are to be forbidden or at least strictly limited, though "they that are foul" are compassionately granted "a greater portion."

With a few minor exceptions, his proposed reforms support one of two main objectives—the restriction of the hereditary transmission of mental illness and the removal, as far as possible, of various social blocks, stresses, and frustrations which subject so many sensitive people to unendurable strains. This was the end of his search. There, in the fields of heredity and environment, lay the

[37] The word for "slums" in Burton's day was "suburbs." The wretched hovels then built against (literally *under*) the cities' walls were usually outside the corporation's jurisdiction, and hence were the haunts of beggars, thieves, prostitutes, and others of the miserably indigent.

[38] *Ibid.*, pp. 89, 187–188, and the whole of "Democritus Junior to the Reader," *ibid.*, pp. 11–104.

deep roots of the disease, and there radical treatment must begin its work. That, at long last, was what "Democritus Junior" had to tell the reader. Melancholy had been anatomized, and its cure, as did its symptoms and its causes, lay in the stuff of life round about us. *Paucis notus, paucioribus ignotus* . . .

Conclusion

IN *The Anatomy of Melancholy* Burton proposed to analyze melancholia, to show its nature, its causes, and its proper treatment. To what extent, in the light of modern psychiatry, can he be said to have been successful?

As an observer of symptoms, he was acute and industrious. His clinical material was small, almost negligible, but his survey of literature for information bearing upon abnormal psychology was, and is, without parallel. He brought into focus, or at least under scrutiny, almost all that had ever been said or thought on the subject in the western world. That this literature almost entirely antedated the seventeenth century was to some extent unfortunate, for it failed to include anatomical and physiological discoveries of the highest importance—such as, to mention the most important, the circulation of the blood. But this was more than compensated for by the fact that in their approach to problems of personality the writers of antiquity, the Middle Ages and, the early Renaissance were free from the inhibitions and limitations that the puritan theology and temper were beginning to impose on the later writers.

Burton is sometimes credulous, and his predilection for the bizarre leads him to include in his description much that is irrelevant or even ridiculous, though the observations of modern psychiatry have confirmed the validity, or at least the possibility, of a great deal of what his contemporaries and successors dismissed as fantastic.

Some of the seeming absurdity of the *Anatomy* may be attributed to the outworn logic of its author's classifications, which classifications, however, he did not invent, but took from the best medical writers of his day; and unsatisfactory as they are, they are no more confusing than other classifications based on outmoded psychologies—David Skae's, for example.[1]

His descriptions are too discursive. Much that he includes—hallucinations, ideas of reference, and other symptoms common in psychotic states—indicates that he did not differentiate "melancholy" as sharply from other forms of mental disturbance as twentieth-century psychiatrists differentiate melancholia.

But, when all such allowances have been made, what remains of his clinical picture is highly creditable. He recognized the widespread nature of the disease, the variety of its manifestations, its irrational character, and, above all, the close relation of the abnormal to the normal. He saw anxiety as the central symptom and perceived the difference between real anxiety and that anxiety determined by feelings of guilt.

In stressing the importance of *excess* as a symptom—gluttony as compared with hunger, for example—he seemed to have some awareness of what are now understood as regressive and compensatory mechanisms.

He perceived that jealousy was an "epitome" of melancholia. He noted that the depressed were aggressive, and distinguished the aggressive and self-aggressive nature of many of their acts—such as suicide. He observed that they were disturbed in their sexual relations, unable to objectify their love. He saw that basic envy and mistrust prevented them from forming pleasant or productive associations with other people, and he was aware of the inner frustrations that defeated all their attempts at accomplishment.

These things he saw all about him and found confirmed in his books, but he found a stronger confirmation and much more information in his own soul. The *Anatomy* is not merely a compendium. Many of his most valuable observations were drawn from intuition, a fact of which he seemed rather proud: "Other men," he boasts, "get their knowledge from books, I mine from melancholizing." He confesses that the writing of the *Anatomy* had a therapeutic value to him; he had "a kind of imposthume" in his

[1] See Zilboorg, *A History of Medical Psychology*, pp. 420–421.

head, he says, of which he was "desirous to be unladen." He makes
no secret of the fact that his interest in melancholy was not im-
personal: "One must needs scratch where it itches," he ruefully
admits.

This frankness is commendable, but unnecessary, for the evidence of his disturbed condition stands out plainly. He makes it
quite clear, in the course of his book, that he had suffered an un-
healable narcissistic injury in his childhood that left him resentful,
envious, scornful of himself and of others. The nature of this trau-
matic experience is made evident in the bitterness with which he
discusses the sufferings of children at the hands of unloving parents
and harsh teachers. Again and again he expresses the disturbed attitudes which are based on deep feelings of being rejected and unloved. From this early disturbance in personal relationships stems
his continual self-depreciation and depreciation of others and his
compensatory arrogance and sense of superiority. His truculence
is only thinly overlaid by assumptions of humility and inferiority.
He is bitter in his attack upon all who have any pretension to status
or privilege and reflects the uncomfortable aspect of his disturbed
feelings in sarcasm, irony, and the caustic quality of his humor.

His disturbed and unhappy feelings about his fellow men extend
in full measure to his fellow women. He complains resentfully of
the celibacy imposed upon University Fellows, but certain of the
attitudes toward women which he expresses would indicate that
celibacy was not imposed upon him solely by external prohibitions.
He goes into ecstasies over women, but his enthusiasm seems to be
the expression of a man who wants to be *able* to love. "I long, but
I may not have." His feeling toward women is hostile or, at best,
highly ambivalent. Love, he admits, is only for those who are free
from conflict, and one does not have to read very far into *The
Anatomy of Melancholy* to see that Robert Burton was not one
of those.

His continual attack on scholars and his contempt for Oxford—
ostensibly the sense of proportion of a man of the world in the
face of pedantic pretensions—carries a suggestion of being a form

of self-destruction; he was attacking himself, attacking what he really was and all that truly mattered to him in life.

The compulsive nature of his character shows plainly in his style and method, wholly apart from the violence of his diatribes and the fury of his onslaughts. He seems compelled by some irresistible urge to pile up adjectives, to accumulate synonyms, to follow every theory and describe every cure, even those he despised. He cannot let any idea go until he, it, the reader, and the language are exhausted.

Such a nature, of course, offered a rich field of introspection to anyone interested in the neurotic personality, but it also imposed certain distortions. Keen as his self-analysis was, Burton did not seem able to recognize, for one thing, the symptomatic significance of the self-depreciation to which he was so prone. He was the dupe of his self-justifications, blind to his own aggressiveness and its import. He perceived (in others) that aggression played an important role, and he perceived (in others) that self-depreciation played an important role; but he did not seem to suspect any relationship between them. Perhaps it would have been unendurably painful for him to explore the possibility of their connection.

So much for his symptomatology, its strength and its weaknesses. In the etiology of melancholy he saw three central factors—heredity, lack of affection in childhood, and sexual frustration, and of these he considered the first the most important. He recognized many other causes, to be sure, but only as contributory.

Modern psychiatry would not disagree with him except as to emphasis and detail. The particular constellation of predisposition, emphasized oral need and frustrating early experiences, are typically present in melancholic individuals. The sexual frustrations of later life, which Burton felt to be causes, are today regarded more as effects, repetitions of the early disappointments, occurring as results of the strongly ambivalent attitudes rooted in them.

What Burton's etiology lacked was a dynamic psychology to which to relate his observations. He failed to perceive the relationship between the neurotic's ambivalence and his disturbed personal relationships. Nor did he recognize that the melancholy individual tends to react toward himself as he does toward external objects, particularly the object of love initially most important to him, showing the same ambivalence toward himself that he does toward others. He saw clearly the indications of self-depreciation that mark the depressive phase of melancholia—the lowness of spirits, the timidity, the sense of unworthiness, and the feeling of being especially marked out for misfortune. And he saw with equal clarity the opposite attitudes which the manic phase elicits—the arrogance, the contempt of others which expresses itself in rudeness and insolence, and the self-exaltation shown in the exaggerated concern which the melancholy manifest in all their own concerns, their extreme touchiness, suspiciousness, resentment over trifles, and so forth. But he had no synthesizing theory with which to bring all these things together in any sort of comprehensible whole.

He recognized, to supply further instances, that anxiety was a universal symptom of melancholia, but he did not recognize its relation to the fear of the loss of love. He perceived the strength of aggressiveness in the melancholy character, but he did not concern himself with its origins. He was aware that the inner frustration which prevents the neurotic from accomplishing what he is capable of is in some way connected with fantasy, but he could state it only in the broadest terms: "they are restrained from accomplishing their desire by some supposed impossibility."

Nonetheless, Burton throws out from time to time certain fragmentary ideas which are fascinating and highly arresting. He did not know how the mind works, but some of his guesses so strikingly foreshadow modern psychology that their long neglect must be regarded as one of the minor marvels of the history of thought.

For instance, in regarding many mental disturbances as extensions or exaggerations of "normal" states he was not only more "modern" than many who came after him but also he was on a track that led to fruitful theories and further valuable observations and, what's more, gave a beneficial direction to his entire therapy; whereas the eighteenth and nineteenth centuries, by regarding mental sicknesses as inexplicable "seizures," really reverted to some-

thing very much like the primitive conception of demoniacal possession, and in so doing entered a psychiatric cul-de-sac.

In his inclination toward a psychological rather than a somato-
logical theory of mental disease, Burton is in accord with most
contemporary psychiatrists, if not with most contemporary physicians.

His statement that melancholy is "a symbolizing disease" is profoundly important, as is also his recognition of the need for a mental
hygiene of parent-child relationship. The great amount of space
that he devotes to the phenomenal rigidity of conscience which
the melancholy display proves that he had sensed something, at
least, of the importance of what is now regarded as one of the
fundamental factors in neurosis.

Interesting, also, is his assertion that "the imagination, inwardly
or outwardly moved, represents to the understanding, not enticements only, to favor the passion, or dislike, but a very intensive
pleasure follows the passion, or displeasure, and the will and reason
are captivated by delighting in it," [2] for here, again, he is really
concerned with the part that fantasy plays.

He is quite modern in his understanding of aggression and in his
perception that it is often directed against ourselves: "every man
[is] the greatest enemy unto himself" and "we study many times
to undo ourselves, abusing those good things which God hath
bestowed upon us, health, wealth, strength, wit, learning, art,
memory, to our own destruction . . . we arm our selves to our
own overthrows; and use reason, art, judgement, all that should
help us, as so many instruments to undo us." [3]

In his conception of the nature of the emotional basis of that
distortion of the imagination which he felt to be the prime dynamic
factor in neurosis he comes excitingly close to elaborating a theory
of the unconscious mind. "Perturbations and passions, which trouble the phantasy," he says, in a passage which has already been
quoted, but which is striking enough to be worth repeating,
"though they dwell between the confines of sense [feeling] and
reason, yet they rather follow sense than reason, because they are

[2] *Anatomy*, pp. 359-360.   [3] *Ibid.*, p. 118.

drowned in corporeal organs of sense. They are commonly reduced into two inclinations, *irascible*, and *concupiscible*." [4]

That is, he seems to assert, the distortion of the imagination
which underlies the neurotic personality (in his own words, which
"misinforms the heart" and so leads to irrational anxiety) springs
from impulses or urges which have their origins beyond the awareness of reasoning perception, impulses and urges which, although
they may direct our conscious actions and thoughts, lie submerged
in the dark abyss of our physical being, and these urges are ultimately, he believes, self-assertion in the forms of anger or sexual
desire. In this connection it might be well to remember that
Freud first studied the role of sexuality in neurosis and later came
to emphasize the role of aggression.

The "modernity" of Burton's therapy is equally striking. With
the exception of the "shock" therapies, there is hardly any treatment now employed to which he does not allude.

His statement that melancholia may be "mitigated and much
eased," but is rarely eradicated is amply borne out by the experience of psychiatrists. People do recover from depressive reactions,
with and without treatment, but there is a tendency toward recur-
rence, particularly when the life situation is such as to touch upon
and activate the central emotional situation that underlies the patient's neurotic conflict. Psychoanalysts do analyze some depressive
patients with a considerable measure of success. Recent and acute
depressive reactions, in particular, often respond readily to psychotherapy. But on the whole an analyst would have less expectation
of success with a severely and chronically depressed patient than he
would with a patient afflicted with any one of several other forms
of psychological disturbance.

The compassion which underlies the *Anatomy* is worthy of emphasis. That Burton was not interested in psychotherapy solely as
an intellectual problem was no doubt due to the suffering that he
himself had endured, but, nonetheless, it colors his view of the
problems of treatment with a humanity which is now regarded as
indispensable to any expectation of success. Pinel is generally cred-

[4] *Ibid.*, p. 224.

ited with being the first psychiatrist to appreciate the necessity for kindness and sympathy in the treatment of the insane and to institute rational methods of treatment. That his regime at the Saltpetrière, in which shackles were removed and some approximations of hospital care were made, is considered a revolutionary milestone in the course of psychiatry serves to mark how completely Burton's plea, a hundred and seventy years earlier, had been ignored. And it also serves to mark, of course, how completely Burton's views are unknown to this day.

In addition to his plea for gentleness and humanity, Burton had many valuable positive ideas concerning the treatment of melancholia. He understood quite clearly that mental disturbances cannot be treated wholly by themselves, as some physical disturbances can be treated; he insisted that the patient's total situation must be taken into consideration—his physical state and constitution, his emotional state and attitudes, his intimate personal relationships, his occupation and other activities, and his social environment. In this insistence he anticipates, to a remarkable degree, the most modern conceptions. Forty years ago he would still have been "radical," for it is only within that time that techniques for systematic and co-ordinated medical, psychological, and social studies of the neurotic or psychotic individual have been incorporated into the procedure of psychiatric clinics.

He further recognized as important in treatment what would now be referred to as the strength of the ego, insisting that the patient may "in some sort correct himself." The patient, he maintained, is not wholly helpless in the grip of his malady; he may choose, to some extent, whether he will give way too far to his morbid tendencies.

Burton appreciated the necessity for activity and companionship—although solitary confinement was the prevailing treatment in his day. He anticipated modern recreational and occupational therapy, but he did not regard them as all-important, relegating them, rather, to a secondary position and placing psychotherapy first.

His conception of the function and role of the psychotherapist is in accord with the best present understanding. He perceived the vast importance of the relation between the patient and the therapist, emphasizing the need for kindness and tolerance on the physician's part and respect and confidence on that of the patient.

He states the qualifications requisite for the therapist in remarkably modern terms. He saw that the therapist must be a physician, in order to minister to the physical disturbances which invariably accompany mental disturbances, but he also saw that he must be a psychologist, since an understanding of the processes of the mind is, in this place, of even more importance than the ability to treat bodily ailments. Striking, indeed, is his insistence that the therapist "must first rectify the passions and perturbations of his own mind." It is an interesting anticipation of the present training procedure for psychoanalysts in which a personal analysis is considered a vital part of preparation.

With regard to the direct patient-therapist relationship, Burton clearly understood the value of what in modern psychotherapy are termed "catharsis" and "abreaction," that is, the discharge of pent-up emotion (and a consequent amelioration of neurotic symptoms) that accompanies the patient's talks with the therapist as, gradually, his recollections uncover his basic conflict.

He seems, also, to have understood the usefulness and the limitations of reassurance. He distinguished emphatically between an interested and encouraging attitude, helpful to the patient, on the part of the psychotherapist, and an attitude of indulgence that would tend, on the contrary, to foster infantile reactions.

He was not sentimentally willing to absolve the patient of all responsibility for his own cure, but insisted, rather, that the patient, as well as the physician, must bring sincere effort to the treatment, must wish to recover, and, if necessary, must make sacrifices in order to do so.

Yet, though Burton knew that the influence of the physician over the patient is the "notable secret" of success in psychotherapy, he did not seem to have any conception of the dynamics of the process. His therapy, like his etiology, lacked a supporting psychology. It is in this, more than in anything else, that he falls short of modern psychiatry. He was aware that "simple narration many times easeth" the distressed mind, but he does not seem to have asked very searchingly why this should be so. He may have asked, of course, and found no answer worth recording, but the discursiveness of the *Anatomy* hardly justifies any such theory of reticence.

It may be that in his failure to search deeply into the "why" of these things, despite his eager curiosity in so much else, Burton was merely displaying a temper of mind different from that which now generally prevails. The thought that it was impertinent, if not actually sacrilegious, to inquire into the mystery of things was formerly very strong. Even so curious a man as Montaigne (whom Burton greatly admired) condemned the searching after causes as presumptuous: "The knowledge of causes doth onely concern him, who hath the conduct of things: Not us, that have but the sufferance of them." [5]

This does not mean that Burton was wholly unaware of the impelling forces of the analytic process. The emphasis that he repeatedly placed on the *emotional* relationship of the physician and his patient indicates an awareness, even if a confused awareness, that there was something involved more than a simple narration. The therapist was plainly, in his opinion, not just a listening post.

His statement that the patient may not know, or at least may be unable to tell, the true cause of his sorrow and, therefore, the therapist must seek for it in his "looks, gestures, motions [and] phantasy" comes so close to the very center of much modern psychotherapy as to be breathtaking. In this passage "motions" seems to have the meaning, now obsolete, "inward promptings or impulses, particularly those of a sexual nature"; [6] while "phantasy" meant "imaginings in general." It is not plain how far he meant the therapist to pursue the patient's imaginings or how much im-

---

[5] *The Essays of Montaigne*, Book III, chap. xi; The Modern Library edition, New York, n.d. The translation is by Florio.

[6] See the 9th meaning of the word "motion" in the Oxford English dictionary. The last recorded use in this sense is there given as 1726. Two of their illustrations will suffice: "mocyons and concupyscences" (1504); "We haue Reason to coole our raging Motions" (1604).

portance he meant him to attach to them, but it is clear that he expected the neurotic's true desires and conflicts to be reflected in his imaginings, and, since they were not obvious to his conscious awareness, they would necessarily have to be presented in some disguise. Perhaps it was here that melancholy showed itself as a "symbolizing" disease.

This does not mean, of course, that he would have been willing to accept as the causes of melancholia some of the desires and conflicts which modern psychiatry believes to lie at the bottom of many mental disturbances, though his objection to them would certainly not have been based on squeamishness, for there was nothing squeamish about the man or his age.

There is, of course, in all studies of this nature, the danger of reading too much into an expression or phrase from some writer of the past. Burton's intellectual achievement is great enough within the bounds of what he makes plainly intelligible, and he has already suffered too much from being praised for the wrong things.

It would be difficult to claim for him any place in the development of psychiatry. Many of his ideas are astonishingly similar to the most modern conceptions, but since the modern ideas were arrived at in complete independence of him—Burton and his writings being as unknown to psychology as his own Didacus Astunica or Sigismundus Scheretzius, he can hardly be said to have contributed anything. At best he can only confirm.

Floyd Dell has called him "a scholarly and humanistic precursor of Freud," [7] and although one who has labored with Burton as long as Dell has is entitled to his enthusiasms, the statement is excessive. For the one thing that Burton lacked was just that synthesizing imagination which distinguishes Freud from his predecessors. Burton had, to be sure, a real awareness of the dynamic character of the relationship between the individual and his social environment, but he remained almost entirely on a descriptive level. Occasionally there are brilliant flashes of intuition which come startlingly close to enunciating certain ideas which Freud is credited with having first conceived; but these flashes are intermittent, and there is

[7] *Anatomy,* p. xiii.

nothing to show that they are part of a co-ordinated whole or that Burton was aware of their full significance. He certainly fore-shadowed some of Freud's contributions to psychology, but he was never even on the verge of Freud's unified and dynamic theory of the structure of the personality.

It would be a more exact compliment, perhaps, to call him a precursor of Havelock Ellis—though the various admirers of the two men might disagree as to which was favored by the compari-son. Like Ellis, Burton was a humanist, bringing to his task great learning and wide interests. Nothing was alien to him that in any way concerned man or his mind. Like Ellis, he was willing to divest himself of prudery and other restrictions in order to see the truth more clearly. Like Ellis, also, he avowedly sought through his work to ameliorate the lot of mankind. Freud, no doubt, sought the same thing and certainly accomplished it to an infinitely greater degree than either Burton or Ellis, but Freud's approach was much more detached and scientific than theirs. Burton was particularly like Ellis in the indefatigability with which he observed and collected the phenomena of morbid psychology, but he was also like Ellis in that he never achieved any pattern of interpretation that would excite and direct further investigation. Description became for both Burton and Ellis almost an end in itself.

On the other hand, as a psychiatrist Burton deserves better than the qualification which Dell attaches to his praise; namely, that in its scientific aspect the *Anatomy* is "merely a quaint curiosity." Burton's starting point, that the difference between the normal and the neurotic is one of degree and the conflicts which the neurotic must solve are basically those which all men must solve, is still val-uable and something of which laymen, at least, are not yet suffi-ciently aware. Much that is included in his symptomatology is, indeed, quaint and curious, but most of this quaint and curious material is quoted from other authors and is not accepted by Bur-ton without reservations. When he writes from his own mind, as Dr. Johnson observed, there is "great spirit and great power in what he says."

His therapy cannot be dismissed as archaic. That he does not understand the why of it may be a defect, but it is not one that invalidates it.

In his perception of the relation of culture and neurosis and his suggestions for social reform he is deserving of the highest praise. From the psychiatric point of view two of his objectives stand out prominently—the restriction of the hereditary transmission of mental disturbances, and the alleviation of certain frustrations inherent in the present structure of society. But his specific suggestions, good as many of them are, are not as significant as the general suggestion of which they are a part. The important thing—and it is very important—is that he saw in cultural determinants the bases for disturbances in personality development and neurotic deviations and felt that in creating such disturbances and deviations society was failing to accomplish its chief objective and should, therefore, be completely reorganized. The utopia which he sketches in his address to the reader—really a summing up of the whole matter—shows how seriously he had accepted the responsibility implicit in his title.

It is true that he has very little to offer the psychologist now. A student of psychiatry would be ill-advised to drudge through his long digressions, or to attempt to disentangle his facts from his fictions, or to seek to impose a modern order upon his archaic structure, merely for his scientific value. All that he has to say about psychology can now be obtained elsewhere with a great deal less effort.

But the social scientist who desires confirmation for his feeling of the need for reform, the philosopher who is interested in the ways in which ideas spread or sometimes fail to spread, and the psychiatrist who seeks to refute the popular charge that much of abnormal psychology is a preposterous and lewd invention of modern psychologists—all these will find the ideas of the "fantastic great old man" most fascinating. For the *Anatomy* serves to remind us how much was actually known three hundred years ago and how carefully some psychopathic states had been observed. That this knowledge seems startling to many people today is due in part to the fact that the past two centuries have been in some respects a period of intellectual retrogression. Modern psychiatry, *The Anatomy of Melancholy* makes abundantly clear, is the continuation of an interrupted process whose origins are almost coeval with any human record.

Bibliography

THIS is a list of biographical and critical works discussing or referring to Burton and *The Anatomy of Melancholy*, with brief comments. *The Cambridge Bibliography of English Literature* lists some ten thousand writers, of whom approximately three thousand may be regarded as "literary" figures. Of these, judging from the number of titles listed in *The Cambridge Bibliography*, less than fifty have been the subject of more critical articles than has Robert Burton, and of single works in English it is questionable if a score have been more written about than *The Anatomy of Melancholy*. Despite all this, hardly any attention whatever has been paid to Burton's avowed purpose in writing the book.

Adams, Edward W. "Robert Burton and the Anatomy of Melancholy," *Gentleman's Magazine*, LVII, 46. Reprinted in *Eclectic Magazine*, CXXVI, 264.
A well-written, humorous appreciation of Burton's style and mannerisms. The pretense of a serious purpose in the *Anatomy* is regarded as one of Burton's jokes.

Aitken, P. Henderson. "The Cypher of Burton's Signature Solved," *Athenaeum*, No. 4426 (Aug. 24, 1912), pp. 193–194.
A short note offering an interesting suggestion as to why Burton "almost always in his books added under his name three *r*'s, arranged in the form of an inverted pyramid."

Aldington, Richard. "Burton the Anatomist," *Nation and Athenaeum*, XXXVI (March 21, 1925), 860–861.
A review of Mead and Clift, *Burton the Anatomist*, which is characterized as "inept . . . uncritical . . . paltry, perfunctory and slipshod."

"Anatomy of Melancholy, The," *Cornhill Magazine*, XLI, 475–490 (April, 1880). Reprinted in *Appleton's Journal*, VIII (June, 1880), 512–521.
Patronizing ("There is real charm in the old gentleman") and worthless.

"Anatomy of Melancholy, The," *Saturday Review*, LXI (May 1, 1886) 613–614.

A review of the Nimmo ed. (3 vols., 1886). It accepts the *Anatomy* as a serious work, but makes no attempt to present or judge its psychiatric material.

"Anatomy of Melancholy, The," *Scottish Review*, VIII (July, 1886), 45–60.

A review of the Nimmo ed. (3 vols., 1886). The author admits that melancholy, "a repellent subject," has "a sort of perennial interest," but demonstrates his own complete immunity from any such concern.

"Anatomy of Melancholy, The," *Spectator*, LIX (June 5, 1886), 750–752.

The author takes advantage of the opportunity offered by a review of the Nimmo ed. (3 vols., 1886) to write an essay on religion as the true cure for despair.

Andrade, E. N. da C. "Master of Melancholy," *New Statesman*, XVI (Oct. 23, 1920), 79–80.

One of the best appreciative essays on Burton. The seriousness of Burton's intent is recognized, but there is no attempt to present his psychiatry.

Aubrey, John. Brief Lives. 2 vols. Oxford, 1898.

Vol. 1, p. 130, contains a brief biographical note communicated to Aubrey by "Mr. Robert Hooke of Greshman College," stating that it was "whispered" in Christ Church that Burton had committed suicide.

Barry, Charles. "Robert Burton's Anatomy of Melancholy," *Bookman's Journal and Print Collector*, XIV (July, 1926), 87–89.

A short, well-written appreciation of Burton's style. No attempt is made to estimate the psychiatric ideas of the *Anatomy*.

Bensly, Edward. "A hitherto unknown source of Montaigne and Burton," *Athenaeum*, No. 4219 (Sept. 5, 1908), p. 270.

A Mr. Jacobs had stated in the *Athenaeum* for June 6, 1908, that Burton had obtained "much of his erudition from Theodore Zwinger, Professor of Medicine at Basel and author of The Theatre of Human Life (1565)." Bensly and Aldis Wright had replied in the issue of June 13, and Bensly here answers more fully, admitting Burton's use of Zwinger, but questioning Jacobs's "much."

—— "Burton's Anatomy of Melancholy," *Notes and Queries*. Series 9, XI–XII; Series 10, I, II–VIII, X–XI (1903–1909), *passim*.

In this series of notes Professor Bensly identifies passages from earlier authors in the *Anatomy* and indicates numerous errors in Shilleto's edition.

—— "Burton and Fletcher," *Notes and Queries*, Series 10, VI (Dec. 15, 1906), 464.

A careful consideration as to whether Burton quoted Fletcher in one passage in the *Anatomy*. The conclusion is that he did not.

—— "Burton and Jacques Ferrand," *Notes and Queries*, Series 10, XI (April 10, 1909), 286.

An alleged source disproved.

—— "Burton's 'Anatomy of Melancholy': Presentation Copy of the First Edition," *Notes and Queries*, Series 10, VIII, XI (1907, 1909), *passim.*

Bullen had asked why Christ Church had no copy of the first edition of the *Anatomy*. Bensly replies that Burton's own autographed copy of this edition, which he had presented to Christ Church, is now in the British Museum. Bensly writes again to say that Whibley had previously called attention to the above fact. He praises Whibley, but corrects several slight inaccuracies in his article on Burton.

—— "Burton in the XVIII Century," *Notes and Queries*, CLXX (Feb. 1, 1936), 87.

Bensly corrects an allusion of Miss Boddy's.

—— "Robert Burton, John Barclay and John Owen," in The Cambridge History of English Literature, IV, 277–290.

This chapter is concerned, as a chapter in *The Cambridge History of English Literature* should be, with the literary aspects of the *Anatomy*. Osler's praise of its medical value is quoted with approval.

—— "Some Alterations and Errors in Successive Editions of the *Anatomy*," in Proceedings, Oxford Bibliographical Society, I, Part 3 (1925), 233–234.

—— "The Title of R. Burton's Anatomy of Melancholy," *Modern Language Review*, IV, 233–234.

A collection of evidence to show that "Anatomy" was a conventional term in the medical works of Burton's day. Against the implications of this is the fact that Burton himself refers to it as a "phantastical" title.

—— "Theodorus Prodromus, John Barclay and Robert Burton." *Notes and Queries*, Series 10, XI (Feb. 6, 1909), 101–102.

A discussion of one of Burton's sources.

Birrell, Augustine. "That Fantastic Great Old Man," *Times Literary Supplement*, No. 1253 (Jan. 21, 1926), pp. 33–34. Reprinted in the *Nation and Athenaeum*, XXXVIII (Feb. 13, 1926), 678–679.

Under pretext of reviewing the Nonesuch edition of the *Anatomy* the author quaintly attempts an essay on Burton in Burton's own style. At least half of the essay—and by far the best half—is made up of quotations from the *Anatomy*.

Boddy, Margaret P. "Burton in the XVIII Century," *Notes and Queries,* CLXVII (Sept. 22, 1934), 206–208.

Miss Boddy demonstrates that the *Anatomy* had a slight influence on the *Spectator.*

—— "Johnson and Burton," London *Times Literary Supplement,* No. 1690 (June 21, 1934), p. 443.

Johnson's facetious definition of "oats" is compared with a similar joke in the *Anatomy.* Dorian (*ibid.,* September 13, 1934, p. 620) thinks Johnson's definition might have come from Fuller's *Worthies.*

Boswell, James. Life of Johnson. ed. G. B. Hill. Oxford, 1887. II, 121, 440; III, 415.

There are only one or two references to Burton in Boswell's *Life.* Johnson states his fondness for the book and praises Burton's wisdom. Johnson seems to have read the *Anatomy* for its medical value, for which he praises it highly.

Bradford, Gamaliel, Jr. "Anatomy of Melancholy; an odd sort of popular book," *Atlantic Monthly,* XCIII (April, 1904), 548–554. Reprinted in Bradford's collection of essays entitled *A Naturalist of Souls,* New York, 1917.

An appreciative essay concerned chiefly with Burton's biography and his style. There is no reference to the psychiatric aspects of the *Anatomy,* except for the statement that Burton's definition of melancholy is too vague and inclusive.

—— "Quaint Old Treatise of Love: Burton's Anatomy of Melancholy," *Sewanee Review,* XIX (April, 1911), 172–184.

A distinct improvement on the earlier essay in the *Atlantic,* though nothing serious is said about the *Anatomy*'s psychiatric value.

Brown, T. E. "Robert Burton (Causerie)," *New Review,* XIII (1895), 257–266.

The Reverend Brown is plainly annoyed with the *Anatomy:* it is a "rueful and most melancholy abuse" of scholarship; its method is "the grossest fooling," and "neglect and decay" are its just reward. He contemptuously accuses Burton of wasting his time in the Christ Church library when he should have been down at the river "cheering the struggling crew" or trying "his own arm at the ponderous sixteenth century oar." The basis of his animus is that Burton was devoid of "principle" in that he obstinately refused to see that the Christian religion offered the sole cure for melancholy.

Bullen, A. H. "Introduction" to the Shilleto ed. of the Anatomy of Melancholy. 3 vols. London, 1893, 1896, 1904, 1923, 1926.

Bullen's essay is biographical and appreciative: "For them that have once fallen under the spell of the *Anatomy* there can be no disenchantment. The marvellous book that charmed their free fancy in youth, will in manhood keep a bower quiet for them amid the turmoil of work-a-day life . . ."

"Burton's Anatomy of Melancholy," *Blackwood's Edinburgh Magazine*, XC (Sept., 1861), 323–342.
A brief summary of the *Anatomy*, with a comment. A good literary criticism. No attention at all paid to the psychiatric value.

"Burton the Anatomist," *Spectator*, No. 5073 (Sept. 19, 1925), p. 451.
A review of Mead and Clift, *Burton the Anatomist*, in which little is said either of Burton or of the edition under review.

Burton, Robert. For a complete bibliography of the editions of *The Anatomy of Melancholy* and Burton's other writings see Chapter V of Paul Jordan-Smith's *Bibliographia Burtoniana*.
For a copy of Burton's will see the Proceedings of the Oxford Bibliographical Society, I, Part 3 (1925), 218–220.

Burton, William. The Description of Leicester Shire. London [1622].
Contains a few items about Burton's family. There is very little, but that very little is all we have.

Byron, George Gordon. Letters and Journals; ed. by R. E. Prothero. London, 1898–1901. II, 383; V, 184, 392. Poetry; ed. by E. H. Coleridge. London, 1898–1904. II, 236. Letters and Journals; with notices of his life, by Thomas Moore. London, 1930. I, 98.
Lord Byron makes one or two trifling, favorable comments on Burton. It is interesting that despite his own neurotic personality he did not seem to suspect the true import of the *Anatomy*, regarding it solely as a collection of learned curiosities.

Curry, J. T. "Robert Burton and His Anatomy of Melancholy," *Gentleman's Magazine*, CCLXXXVIII, No. 2030 (Feb., 1900), 185–203.
A biographical sketch, the materials for which are drawn, as fully as possible, from the *Anatomy*. Burton's claim to be writing a serious medical treatise is dismissed as absurd.

Cushing, Harvey W. Life of Sir William Osler. 2 vols. New York and London, 1925.
There are sixteen references to Burton in the course of this work, trifling individually, but attesting collectively to Osler's great interest in the *Anatomy*. Of especial interest is the fact that he planned to write an introduction to Burton's great work stressing its importance as a medical treatise.

Dawson, W. J., and C. W. Dawson. "Robert Burton—Remedies of Discontents," in Great English Essayists, New York, 1909, pp. 31–35.
In an anthology of English essayists the Dawsons, editors, include four pages of selections from the *Anatomy*.

Dell, Floyd. "Introduction" (pp. xiii–xiv), in his edition of the *Anatomy*, New York, 1927.
Pays brief tribute to Burton as "a scholarly and humanistic precursor of Freud."
—— "Keats's Debt to Burton," *Bookman*, LXVII (March, 1928), 13–17.
A summary of what was already known plus the interesting suggestion that the central idea of the "Ode on Melancholy" is also taken from the *Anatomy*.

Dieckow, Fritz. John Florios englische Übersetzung der Essais Montaigne's und Lord Bacon's, Ben Jonson's und Robert Burton's Verhältnis zu Montaigne. Strassburg, 1903.
"Wir sehen: Wie auf die Werke Bacon's und Ben Jonson's so ist auch auf die 'Anatomy' des Robert Burton ein deutlich wahrnehmbarer Einfluss von Montaigne's Essais ausgegangen, ein Einfluss, der bei Burton umso erklärlicher und stärker erschient, als dieser Gelehrte in Neigung und Charakter am meisten, mehr als Jonson und Bacon, Montaigne ähnelt" (p. 115). Pages 92–115 of this dissertation are devoted to Burton. They consist entirely of passages from the *Anatomy* and passages from the *Essais* that are similar in thought or phrasing. Few of them are close enough to prove direct borrowing.

Duff, Edward Gordon. "The Fifth Edition of Burton's Anatomy of Melancholy," *Library*, IV (1923), 81–102.
An account of the manner in which the fifth edition of the *Anatomy* was printed—partly in London, partly in Oxford, and partly in Edinburgh.

Duff, Edward Gordon, and F. Madan. "Notes on the Bibliography of the Oxford editions of the *Anatomy*," in Proceedings Oxford Bibliographical Society, I, Part 3 (1925), 191–197.

Ewing, S. B., Jr. "Burton, Ford and Andromana," PMLA, LIV (Dec., 1939), 1007–1017.
The author maintains that John Ford's studies in abnormal psychology were "based on the case histories in Burton's *Anatomy*." On the strength of parallel passages he seeks to prove that Ford was the author of *Andromana*. The essay is of more interest to students of Ford than to students of Burton.

Ferriar, John. Illustrations of Sterne: with other essays and verses. 2d ed. London, 1812.
Ferriar presents conclusive evidence for his conviction that most of the singularities of Walter Shandy "were drawn from the perusal of Burton" who furnished "the grand magazine" for Sterne's borrowing. The book—despite the fact that Ferriar was himself a physician and interested in the vagaries of the mind—makes no effort to consider the *Anatomy*'s

medical value. Nonetheless it is curious and interesting. Ferriar points out, for example, that the very passage in *Tristram Shandy* in which Sterne attacks plagiary is plagiarized from the *Anatomy*. And he further shows (see p. 99) how far Sterne went out of his way to conceal his borrowings. That such extensive filching could pass completely unnoticed shows how deeply Burton had sunk into oblivion by the middle of the eighteenth century.

Finger, Charles J. The Gist of Burton's "Anatomy of Melancholy." Girard, Kans., 1924.
An essay (about 15,000 words) on Burton and kindred spirits. Its chief emphasis is on Burton's criticism of certain social evils.

Fox, Arthur W. "Robert Burton," in his A Book of Bachelors, Westminster, 1899, pp. 398–436.
A biographical study. The author is inclined to believe that Burton did commit suicide.

Fry, Roger. "The Anatomy of Melancholy, by Democritus Jr.," *Dial*, LXXXI (August, 1926), 142–147.
Fry takes the occasion of reviewing the Nonesuch ed. of the *Anatomy* to discuss the relationship of illustrations to the book they are presumed to illustrate. His prediction of a "unique and distinguished position" for this ed. of the *Anatomy* was at variance with the opinions of most of the other reviewers. The essay has practically nothing to do with Burton or his ideas.

Fuller, Thomas. The Worthies of England. London, 1662. Part 2, p. 134.
A brief biographical notice, hardly ten lines in all, stating that Burton himself suffered from melancholy and that the *Anatomy* had a large sale.

Gibson, S., and F. R. D. Needham. "Two Lists of Burton's Books," in Proceedings Oxford Bibliographical Society, I, Part 3 (1925), 222–246.
Lists of Burton's books received by the Bodleian and by Christ Church library under Burton's will.

Hearne, Thomas. Reliquiae Hearnianae; the Remains of Thomas Hearne, M.A., of Edmund Hall, ed. by Philip Bliss. Oxford, 1857.
Hearne makes two brief references to Burton. He tells the story of his impertinence to the Earl of Southampton, states that the reputation of his charm in conversation still lingered in Oxford, and comments sadly on the neglect into which the *Anatomy* had fallen.

Herring, Thomas. Letters to William Duncombe. London, 1777.
In one letter there is a passing reference to Burton as, of all authors, "the pleasantest, the most learned, and the most full of sterling sense." And it is interesting that this commendation was elicited from the Archbishop by Burton's condemnation of publishing sermons as a means to ecclesiastical preferment.

Hiscock, W. G. "Burton's Anatomy," *Times Literary Supplement*, No. 1633 (May 18, 1933), p. 348.
A minute typographical note.

Holmes, Oliver Wendell. "Pillow-Smoothing Author," *Atlantic Monthly*, LI (April, 1883), 457.
Though himself a physician, Holmes pays no attention whatever to Burton's profession of a serious medical purpose. He chooses, rather, to emulate Burton's discursiveness and to be quaint. He advances some—not very convincing—claims of Burton's influence on the phrasing of other authors and amuses himself (quite needlessly) by speculating as to whether or not Burton was married.

Hughes, Merritt Y. "Burton on Spenser," PMLA, XLI (1926), 545–567.
The author's thesis is that in writing the *Anatomy* Burton was "unconsciously" annotating Spenser's *Faerie Queene*.

Johnson, Samuel. Letters; ed. by G. B. Hill. 2 vols. Oxford, 1893.
Vol. I, pp. 293, 383, contain brief praises of the *Anatomy* in passing. They are of no value except to confirm Johnson's high opinion of Burton.

Jordan-Smith, Paul. "Introduction" (pp. ix–xiii) in the edition of the *Anatomy* ed. by Floyd Dell and Jordan-Smith. New York, 1927.
Chiefly biographical.

—— Bibliographia Burtoniana; a study of Robert Burton's The Anatomy of Melancholy, with a bibliography of Burton's writings. Stanford, 1931.
An entertaining and scholarly account of Burton, the *Anatomy*, its various editions, sources, and those who borrowed from it. No attempt is made to discuss or evaluate its psychiatry.

Jusserand, J. J. Histoire littéraire du peuple anglais. 2 vols. Paris, 1894–1904. Trans. into English in 3 vols. 1895–1909.
Vol. 3, pp. 502–509, contains a brief essay on the literary merits of the *Anatomy*.

Lake, Bernard. A General Introduction to Charles Lamb; with a Special Study of His Relation to Robert Burton. Leipzig, 1903.
A study of the influence of Burton's style on Lamb's.

Lamb, Charles, and Mary Lamb. Works; ed. by E. V. Lucas. 7 vols. London, 1903–1905.
In the Letters (VI, 159, 161, 173) there are passing mentions of the *Anatomy*. In I, 175, 452; II, 40, 67, 174; and V, 27, 29, there are passing mentions of Burton. He is praised, and there is one essay in humorous imitation of his style.

Ll[uelyn], M[artin]. "Elegie: on the Death of Master R. B." in Men-Miracles; with Other Poemes, London, 1656.

A brief tribute, hardly even of biographical interest.

Lowes, John Livingston. "The Loveres Maladye of Hereos," *Modern Philology*, XI (April, 1914), 1–56.
Professor Lowes surveys the medical lore of ten centuries to show that "Hereos" (Burton's Love Melancholy) is derived etymologically from Eros. It is to be regretted that Professor Lowes has never found time to write, as he once hoped to, on the medical aspects of the *Anatomy*, for he, almost alone of modern scholars, would be capable of treating the subject adequately.

Macray, W. D. Annals of the Bodleian Library. Oxford, 1890.
Information concerning Burton's books.

Mead, G. C. F., and Rupert C. Clift, ed. Burton the Anatomist; with a Preface by W. H. D. Rouse. New York, 1925.
The Preface is biographical and appreciative. The work is composed chiefly of excerpts from the *Anatomy* and despite its professed intent of displaying Burton's meaning, has little value.

Melancholy Anatomized, London, 1865.
A version of the *Anatomy* that comes very close to being *Hamlet* without the Prince of Denmark. It has been bowdlerized, condensed, and all quotations have been deleted. A Preface claims that the purpose of Burton's work was to show young people the value of temperance, restraint, and chastity and to convince them that "perfect serenity of mind may . . . be completely preserved by a life devoted to the practice of real virtue and true religion."

Miller, Joseph L. "Burton's Anatomy of Melancholy," *Annals of Medical History*, VIII (1936), 44–53.
A brief summary which acknowledges the medical value of the *Anatomy*, but makes no effort to appraise it in the light of modern psychiatry.

Murry, John Middleton. "Burton's Anatomy of Melancholy," *Times Literary Supplement*, No. 1006 (April 28, 1921), 265–266. Reprinted in *Living Age*, CCCIX (June 4, 1921), 589–597. Reprinted as "Burton's 'Anatomy' " in Murry's collection of Essays entitled *Countries of the Mind*, First Series, Oxford, 1931.
A fine essay, praising Burton's "practical wisdom and humanity" and his "fine, magnanimous spirit." A shrewd & sympathetic analysis of Burton's character, high praise for his utopia, but no specific consideration of his psychiatry.

Newton, A. Edward. "Burton's Anatomy and Another," in End Papers, Boston, 1933, pp. 95–103.
Contains neither facts nor opinions concerning Burton's life, style, or psychiatry.

Nichols, John. Illustrations of the Literary History of the Eighteenth Century. London, 1822.
Vol. IV, p. 210, contains a trivial mention in passing of the *Anatomy*.
—— The History and Antiquities of the County of Leicester. 8 vols. London, 1797–1815.
Vol. III, pp. 415–419, 557–559, 1137, and Vol. IV, pp. 635, 668, contain biographical materials.
Osler, Sir William. "Burton's Anatomy of Melancholy," *Yale Review*, III (Jan., 1914), 251–271.
Although this essay deals chiefly with Burton's life and the literary merits of the *Anatomy*, it is noteworthy for the emphatic manner in which the medical value of the work is stressed. Unfortunately, however, Osler did not illustrate or enlarge upon his statement that the *Anatomy* was "the greatest medical treatise ever written by a layman." Perhaps this was because he intended to treat the subject at length in a separate essay.
—— "Burton, the Man, His Book, His Library," in Proceedings Oxford Bibliographical Society, I (1925), 163–190.
This is an expansion of the ideas expressed in the *Yale Review* in 1914. Again there is a vigorous emphasis on the medical value of the *Anatomy*, but again there is no illustration of the statement.
—— "Extract from . . . Remarks Made by Sir William Osler at the Opening of the Bodleian Shakespeare Tercentenary Exhibition, April 24, 1916," in Proceedings Oxford Bibliographical Society, I (1925), 216–218.
Osler speaks of Burton as one of the great "transmitters" of learning. Only "the golden compilation" of the *Anatomy* survives of all the medieval encyclopaedias. At the conclusion is the interesting statement that there are, or were, those who claimed Burton as the author of the plays popularly attributed to Shakespeare. For further information on *that* subject see an article by George Parker in the Bodleian *Quarterly Record*, II, 102.
Phelps, W. L. "As I See It," *Scribner's Magazine*, LXXXVII (Feb., 1930), 221.
Professor Phelps quotes a criticism of the *Anatomy*, wherein it is compared to a cathedral, written by one of his undergraduate students thirty years earlier.
Popenoe, Paul. "Robert Burton, Eugenist," *Eugenics Review*, XXIX (July, 1937), 153.
The writer, a member of the Institute of Family Relations, Los Angeles, California, quotes Burton's proposed eugenic reforms from Part 1, sec. 2, memb. 1, subs. 1, of the *Anatomy*.

Powys, Llewelyn. "Robert Burton," in Rats in the Sacristy, London. [1937], pp. 185–195.

One of the best of the appreciative essays.

Reed, Amy L. The Background for Gray's Elegy; a study in the taste for melancholy poetry, 1700–1751. New York, 1924. "Columbia University Studies in English and Comparative Literature."

Chapter I summarizes the *Anatomy* as a beginning of an understanding of the meaning attributed to the word "melancholy" in the early eighteenth century.

"Robert Burton and the Anatomy of Melancholy," *All the Year Round*, LXX (Feb. 27, 1892), 199–202.

An appreciative and mildly patronizing discussion of the *Anatomy* and its author. No comment on the book's medical purpose or value.

Smith, C. C. "The Anatomy of Melancholy," *Christian Examiner*, LXVIII (March, 1860), 211.

Largely a summary; makes no attempt to consider it as a work of psychiatry.

Squire, J. C. "Burton's Anatomy," in Essays at Large, New York [1922], pp. 83–87.

A short and amusing appreciation of Burton's style, wisdom, and humor.

Warton, Thomas, ed. Poems upon Several Occasions by John Milton. London, 1785.

In a footnote (p. 93) Warton asserts that Milton borrowed the idea of *L'Allegro* and *Il Penseroso* "together with some particular thoughts, expressions, and rhymes, more especially the idea of a contrast between these two . . . from a fragmentary poem prefixed to the first edition of Burton's *Anatomy of Melancholy*."

Wendell, Barrett. "Development of Prose: Ralegh, Burton and Browne," in Temper of the Seventeenth Century in English Literature, New York, 1904, pp. 184–206.

A light essay which concerns itself chiefly with Burton's biography and the extent of his learning. No attention is paid to the psychiatric value of the *Anatomy*.

Whibley, Charles. "Robert Burton," in Literary Portraits, New York, 1920.

A long appreciative essay. The author refuses to take the medical pretensions of the *Anatomy* seriously.

White, Kennett. A Register and Chronicle. London, 1728.

It is to a marginal note on pp. 320–321 of Vol. I of this work that we owe our knowledge of Burton's laughing at the profanity of the bargees. White adds that "he was suspected to be Felo de se."

124   *Bibliography*

Wood, Anthony. *Athenae Oxonienses*, 2nd ed. London, 1721.
  The *Athenae* is the source of most of the biographical material that is not drawn directly from the *Anatomy*.
Zilboorg, Gregory, and George W. Henry. A History of Medical Psychology. New York, 1941.
  Burton is mentioned in a footnote, but there is no seeming awareness that the *Anatomy* was intended as a serious psychiatric work.

Index

128   *Index*

Melancholy, of Democritus (*Cont.*)
47; difficulty of defining and dealing with subject, 47 f.; recognized as "a symbolizing disease," 48, 62, 103; as extensions or exaggerations of normal states, 49 f., 61, 102, 109; symptoms, 49-62, 99-101; anxiety the central symptom, 50 f., 99, 102, 104; counsel and comfort wasted upon: imagination at fault, 52, 80; social relationships: thinking capacity, 52; other characteristics, 52 ff., 80; relation to physical conditions, 56, 63, 69, 88, 105; a disease of both soul and body, 56; pleasant aspects: insufferable anguish, 59; distinguished from other psychopathic states, 62, 99; causes of, 63-77, 91, 101-4; supernatural origin: demonology, 65 ff.; "nonnatural" causes, 69; important cause is *inward*: others are contributory, 70; basic causes, 71, 76, 87, 101; heredity, 71, 96, 101, 110; mitigated but rarely eradicated, 78, 91, 104; "unlawful" and absurd remedies, 78, 81; treatment, 78-91, 104-10; dreadful treatment in public institutions: sensitivity and aliveness to suffering, 80; physician-patient relationship, 80, 87-91, 106 f.; no specific remedy: an individual matter, 81; medicines, stimulants, and narcotics, 82; avoidance of all conditions and situations tending to excite it, 84; need for occupation and diversion, 84, 86, 105; for cleanliness, 86; the basic cure must include means of controlling the imagination: need of an external fixed point of reference, 87; recognized late, treatment long, 88; desire to be cured, and other qualities required in patient, 90; origin in circumstances and social environment, 91; prevention a matter of remodeling the structure of society, 91-97; appraisal of Burton's analysis, 99 ff.; consideration of patient's total situation, 105

Mental disease, interest in, during Burton's time, 44; curable and incurable types, 78; cruel treatment in asylums, 80; restriction of hereditary transmission, 96, 110
Miller, Joseph, 46
Miscellanies (Aubrey), 68
Montaigne, (Michel de) 107
Moral scruples, 57
Murry, J. Middleton, quoted, 19
Mystery and gullibility in preNewtonian world, 64

Names, medieval custom of latinizing, 29
Narcotics and stimulants, 82
Nubrigensis, 36

Occupational therapy, 84 f., 105
Ode on Melancholy (Keats), 44
Osler, Sir William, 46
Oxford, 7, 100; Christ Church, 4, 7, 10, 12

Paracelsus, 68
Parent-child relationship, 6, 71, 100, 103
Persius, 18
Perturbations and passions, 69, 87, 103
Philosophaster (Burton), 10
Phlebotomy, 78
Physical conditions, relation to mental condition, 56, 63, 69, 88, 105
Physicians, Latinized names, 30; amount of attention given *The Anatomy*, 45; outstanding innovators, 63; obtuse exhortations, 80; why best fitted for role of friend, 88; qualifications needed, 88 ff., 106; personal influence the secret of successful cures, 90
Physiology and anatomy, established concepts, 63
Pied Piper, 39
Pinel, Philippe, 104
Pomponatius of Padua (Pomponazzi), 29
Prevention must deal with circumstances and environment: social reform, 91-97

WITHDRAWN